Cliffs

D1045800

Jacobs'
Incidents in the Life of a Slave Girl

By Durthy A. Washington

IN THIS BOOK

- Learn about the Life and Background of the Author

- Preview an Introduction to the Novel

- Explore themes, character development, and recurring images in the Critical Commentaries

- Examine in-depth Character Analyses

- Acquire an understanding of the novel with Critical Essays

- Reinforce what you learn with CliffsNotes Review

- Find additional information to further your study in CliffsNotes Resource Center and online at www.cliffsnotes.com.

IDG Books Worldwide, Inc.
An International Data Group Company
Foster City, CA • Chicago, IL • Indianapolis, IN • New York, NY

About the Author

Durthy A. Washington has published numerous articles, essays, and book reviews. She lives in Colorado Springs, Colorado, where she currently serves as English Instructor and Writing Center Director at the U.S. Air Force Academy.

Publisher's Acknowledgments

Editorial

Project Editor: Linda Brandon
Acquisitions Editor: Greg Tubach
Senior Copy Editor: Susan Diane Smith
Editorial Administrator: Michelle Hacker
Glossary Editors: The editors and staff at Webster's New World Dictionaries

Production

Indexer: York Production Services, Inc.
Proofreader: York Production Services, Inc.
IDG Books Indianapolis Production Department

LIMIT OF LIABILITY/DISCLAIMER OF WARRANTY: THE PUBLISHER AND AUTHOR HAVE USED THEIR BEST EFFORTS IN PREPARING THIS BOOK. THE PUBLISHER AND AUTHOR MAKE NO REPRESENTATIONS OR WARRANTIES WITH RESPECT TO THE ACCURACY OR COMPLETENESS OF THE CONTENTS OF THIS BOOK AND SPECIFICALLY DISCLAIM ANY IMPLIED WARRANTIES OF MERCHANTABILITY OR FITNESS FOR A PARTICULAR PURPOSE. THERE ARE NO WAR-RANTIES WHICH EXTEND BEYOND THE DESCRIPTIONS CONTAINED IN THIS PARAGRAPH. NO WARRANTY MAY BE CREATED OR EXTENDED BY SALES REPRESENTATIVES OR WRITTEN SALES MATERIALS. THE ACCURACY AND COM-PLETENESS OF THE INFORMATION PROVIDED HEREIN AND THE OPINIONS STATED HEREIN ARE NOT GUARAN-TEED OR WARRANTED TO PRODUCE ANY PARTICULAR RESULTS, AND THE ADVICE AND STRATEGIES CONTAINED HEREIN MAY NOT BE SUITABLE FOR EVERY INDIVIDUAL. NEITHER THE PUBLISHER NOR AUTHOR SHALL BE LIABLE FOR ANY LOSS OF PROFIT OR ANY OTHER COMMERCIAL DAMAGES, INCLUDING BUT NOT LIMITED TO SPECIAL, INCIDENTAL, CONSEQUENTIAL, OR OTHER DAMAGES.

Table of Contents

How to Use This Book

CliffsNotes Jacobs' *Incidents in the Life of a Slave Girl* supplements the book edited by Jean Fagan Yellin (Harvard University Press, 1987), giving you background information about the author, an introduction to the novel, a graphical character map, critical commentaries, expanded glossaries, and a comprehensive index. CliffsNotes Review tests your comprehension of the original text and reinforces learning with identify the quote, essay questions, and more. For further information on Harriet Jacobs and *Incidents in the Life of a Slave Girl*, check out the CliffsNotes Resource Center.

CliffsNotes provides the following icons to highlight essential elements of particular interest:

Reveals the underlying themes in the work.

Helps you to more easily relate to or discover the depth of a character.

Uncovers elements such as setting, atmosphere, mystery, passion, violence, irony, symbolism, tragedy, foreshadowing, and satire.

Enables you to appreciate the nuances of words and phrases.

Don't Miss Our Web Site

Discover classic literature as well as modern-day treasures by visiting the CliffsNotes Web site at www.cliffsnotes.com. You can obtain a quick download of a CliffsNotes title, purchase a title in print form, browse our catalog, or view online samples.

You'll also find interactive tools that are fun and informative, links to interesting Web sites, tips, articles, and additional resources to help you, not only for literature, but for test prep, finance, careers, computers, and the Internet too. See you at www.cliffsnotes.com!

LIFE AND BACKGROUND OF THE AUTHOR

Personal Background

"God . . . gave me a soul that burned for freedom and a heart nerved with determination to suffer even unto death in pursuit of liberty."

In this excerpt from a letter written by Harriet Jacobs to her friend, the abolitionist Amy Post, Jacobs expresses her determination to continue her quest for freedom. Dated October 9, 1853—less than two years after Jacobs was freed—the letter was written in response to Post's suggestion that Jacobs tell the story of her abuse and exploitation as an enslaved black woman. Eight years later, in 1861—the same year that marked the beginning of the Civil War—*Incidents in the Life of a Slave Girl, Written by Herself* was published in Boston. According to the chronology of Jacobs's life compiled by her autobiographer, Jean Fagan Yellin, the events described in *Incidents* narrated by "Linda Brent" mirror key incidents of Jacobs' life.

Early Years

Harriet Ann Jacobs was born at Edenton, North Carolina, in 1813 to Delilah, the daughter of Molly Horniblow (Aunt Martha), the slave of Margaret Horniblow, and to Daniel Jacobs, a carpenter, the slave of Dr. Andrew Knox. When she was only six years old, Jacobs' mother died, and Jacobs was taken into the household of her mistress, Margaret Horniblow, who taught her to read, spell, and sew. When she was 12, Margaret Horniblow died and willed Harriet to her five-year-old niece, Mary Matilda Norcom (Miss Emily). As a result, Harriet and her brother, John S. Jacobs (William) moved into the household of Dr. James Norcom (Dr. Flint). Shortly after Jacobs' arrival to the Norcom house, her father dies. Feeling sad and alone, Jacobs' life is made even more unbearable by Norcom's determination to make her his concubine. Desperate to escape Norcom, Jacobs entered into a sexual relationship with Samuel Tredwell Sawyer (Mr. Sands) at age 15, with whom she had two children: Joseph and Louisa Matilda (Ben and Ellen).

Undaunted, Norcom continued to pursue Jacobs. When she repeatedly rejected his advances, he sends her to work on a plantation several miles from Edenton. Secure in the knowledge that her children are safe with her grandmother, Jacobs adjusts to plantation life, but when she learns that Norcom plans to send her children to the plantation, she runs away, hiding out at the homes of friends, both black and white. Thinking she has escaped, Norcom sells Jacobs' children and brother to a slave trader, unaware that he is acting on behalf of Sawyer, who allows them to return to Jacobs' grandmother's house. Determined to be near her children, Jacobs spends seven years hiding in her grandmother's attic, where she passes the time sewing and reading the Bible.

After the Escape

Between 1838 and 1842, three events occurred that convinced Jacobs to escape. Sawyer took Louisa Matilda to Washington, D.C., to live with him and his new wife, Lavinia Peyton, and then sends her to his cousins in Brooklyn, New York. Jacobs' brother John ran away from Sawyer, his master. Aunt Betty (Aunt Nancy) died, plunging her grandmother into near-inconsolable grief at the loss of her daughter. Following her escape, Jacobs spent several years as a fugitive slave, alternately living in Boston and New York and supporting her children by working as a seamstress.

In 1849, Jacobs moved to Rochester, New York, where she helped her brother run an antislavery reading room, office, and bookstore in the same building that also housed the offices of Frederick Douglass' newspaper, *The North Star*. In Yellin's "Introduction" to her 1987 edition of *Incidents*, she notes that "the breadth of the references to literature and current events in *Incidents* suggests that during her eighteen months in Rochester [Jacobs] read her way through the abolitionists' library of books and papers" which included "the latest and best works on slavery and other moral questions." During this time, Jacobs also began working with a group of antislavery feminists, which led to her meeting with the abolitionist Amy Post. Post became one of her closest friends and encouraged her to publish her story, despite her understandable reluctance to reveal her painful private life to the public.

Career Highlights

Although Jacobs escaped from slavery at age 27, she did not write her book until nearly 10 years later, following numerous attempts to gain support for the publication of her manuscript. She had initially sought support from Harriet Beecher Stowe, who had gained renown with her publication of *Uncle Tom's Cabin*. But instead of helping her, Stowe offered to include Jacobs' story in her book, *The Key to Uncle Tom's Cabin*. Disappointed and determined to tell her own story, Jacobs began compiling her narrative in 1853, completing it in 1858.

After traveling to Boston to obtain letters to abolitionists abroad, she sailed to England to sell her book. She was unsuccessful, and she returned home and approached Boston publisher, Phillips and Sampson, who agreed to accept the manuscript, and then went bankrupt. Undaunted, Jacobs sent her manuscript to Thayer and Eldridge, another Boston publisher, who agreed to publish it on the condition that it included a preface from Lydia Maria Child. Jacobs' friend, William C. Nell, introduced Jacobs to Child, who agreed to write the preface and act as Jacobs' editor. Shortly after the contract is signed (with Child acting for Jacobs), Thayer and Eldridge also went bankrupt.

At this point, Jacobs decided to purchase the plates of her book and publish it herself. It was finally published in 1861 by a third Boston printer. In 1862, the English edition, *The Deeper Wrong*, was published in London.

Public Service

Following the publication of her book, which received little public acclaim until it was rediscovered more than 100 years later as part of the new renaissance of black women writers, Jacobs spent the remaining years of her life as an activist, supporting herself by working as a seamstress and later running a boarding house in Cambridge, Massachusetts. After her brother's death in 1875, Jacobs and her daughter moved to Washington, D.C., where Louisa Matilda, following her mother's example, helped organize meetings of the National Association of Colored Women. Jacobs died on March 7, 1897, in Washington, D.C. She is buried in Mount Auburn Cemetery in Cambridge.

Achievements

In addition to the extraordinary incidents of her life as a heroic woman who fought for—and won—freedom for herself and her two children, one of the most intriguing aspects of Jacobs' life revolves around her relationship with her editor, Child, who was frequently cited as the "real" author of Jacobs' book by critics who believed that Jacobs' style was too sophisticated for a former slave who lacked formal education. But Child insisted that she did very little editing, crediting Jacobs with authorship of the manuscript. As further evidence that Jacobs wrote the narrative in her own words, Yellin cites numerous letters written by Jacobs, which exemplify an identical style. By encountering skepticism concerning the originality of her work, Jacobs—who is credited to be the first black woman to write a book-length narrative—suffered the same criticism as her predecessor Phillis Wheatley (1753–1784), the first black woman to publish a book of poetry. Today, critics point out that, due to their lack of models and the freedom to develop their own author voice, both women simply emulated the writing style of white authors popular at the time.

Harriet Jacobs was one of the few ex-slaves to write his or her own slave narrative. She was a heroic woman and a loving and fiercely protective mother. She was a writer and activist who fought for the rights of all women.

As a woman who—after spending 27 years in slavery—lived a full, active life until her death at the age of 84, her life stands as a testament to women everywhere who struggle for freedom and survival, demand dignity and respect, and refuse to settle for less than equal representation and full participation in society.

INTRODUCTION TO THE NOVEL

Introduction

"Reader it is not to awaken sympathy for myself that I am telling you truthfully what I suffered. I do it to kindle a flame of compassion in your hearts for my sisters who are still in bondage."

With these words, Harriet Jacobs, speaking through her narrator, Linda Brent, reveals her reasons for deciding to make her personal story of enslavement, degradation, and sexual exploitation public. Although generally ignored by critics, who often dismissed Jacobs' *Incidents in the Life of a Slave Girl, Written by Herself* as a fictionalized account of slavery, the work is heralded today as the first book-length narrative by an ex-slave that reveals the unique brutalities inflicted on enslaved women. As such, it is often cited as the counterpart to the *Narrative of the Life of Frederick Douglass, An American Slave, Written by Himself.*

Authenticity of the Novel

First published in 1861, *Incidents* was "discovered" in the 1970s and reprinted in 1973 and 1987. Since then, several editions of *Incidents* have been published. The most complete and comprehensive version of the narrative is the 1987 Harvard University Press edition, edited by Jacobs' biographer, Jean Fagan Yellin, a professor at New York's Pace University. (The second edition is scheduled for release in April 2000.) In addition to her efforts to establish the authenticity of Jacobs' narrative, Yellin also brought *Incidents* to the attention of readers, scholars, and critics who had long ignored or dismissed the work because it failed to meet the standards of the male slave narrative, as defined by male critics such as Robert Stepto and James Olney.

Scholars who dismissed the work as a fictional slave narrative often pointed out issues such as the following.

Unlike conventional slave narratives, *Incidents* does not acknowledge Harriet Jacobs as its author. Instead, the narrative was published under the pseudonym "Linda Brent."

The narrative's formal, sometimes melodramatic style that emulates the style of 19th century romantic novels seemed totally inappropriate for its "delicate" subject matter: the sexual abuse of enslaved black women.

Its stranger-than-fiction account of a woman who spends seven years hiding in her grandmother's attic to escape her master's insatiable lust seemed too fantastic to be believed.

The primary goal of slave narratives was to arouse sympathy among whites and gain their support for the anti-slavery movement led by abolitionists. Because the publication of *Incidents* coincided with the beginning of the Civil War, it was seen as being published too late to have any social or political impact.

The majority of slave narratives were written by men who documented their daring escapes and heroic actions, many of whom—such as Frederick Douglass—went on to become spokespersons or political leaders. In contrast, Jacobs' story—which focused primarily on her family—was viewed as less important than the stories of her male counterparts.

Male narratives generally followed a strictly chronological format, focusing on the narrator's life as he relates the story of his journey from slavery to freedom. In contrast, Jacobs' narrative focuses on "incidents" in her life. Moreover, instead of following a strictly chronological pattern, Jacobs often interrupts her narrative to address social or political issues such as the church and slavery or the impact of the Fugitive Slave Law on runaways. Consequently, her narrative did not fit the pattern of the "authentic" (male) narrative.

However, Yellin's discovery of letters documenting the correspondence between Jacobs and several prominent 19th century figures—including abolitionist Amy Post, author Harriet Beecher Stowe, and Jacobs' editor Lydia Maria Child—has established the authenticity of Jacobs' narrative and distinguished it as one of the most powerful and courageous works of its time.

For contemporary readers, skepticism generally revolves around the use of language. Critics have pointed out that Jacobs' narrative often depicts Linda as the tragic heroine of British romance novels rather than as an enslaved black woman fighting for survival. They also note that Dr. Flint is sometimes depicted more like a suitor or persistent lover determined to win the hand of his "lady," rather than as a slave owner determined to hold on to his "property."

Readers may also get this idea because Linda, rather than trying to escape, chooses to have two children by Mr. Sands, another white man, a decision that she sees as the lesser of two evils. So readers may conclude that she contributes to her own bondage. Thus, although she uses her sexuality to try to escape her fate, she is ultimately trapped by it.

In many ways, the structure of *Incidents* is similar to that of Samuel Richardson's *Pamela; or, Virtue Rewarded*, an epistolary novel (a novel written in the form of letters) published in 1740 and based on a story about a servant who avoided seduction and was rewarded by marriage. It also bears some similarities to Charlotte Bronte's *Jane Eyre*, first published in 1847 under the pseudonym Currer Bell.

In this novel, Jane, the governess to a ward of the mysterious Mr. Rochester, falls in love with her employer, only to discover that he is already married, and that his wife, who is insane, is confined in the attic of his estate. Jane leaves, but is ultimately reunited with Mr. Rochester after the death of his wife. In one of the most famous quotes from the novel, Jane, an orphan who has survived several miserable years at a charity school, proclaims triumphantly, "Reader, I married him." For Linda, as for other black women, marriage as a means of escape from life's brutalities was not an option. Notably—even though she remains hidden in her grandmother's garret for seven years—she does not become "the madwoman in the attic." In fact, she not only maintains her sanity, but also uses her mind to outwit Dr. Flint, beating him at his own game of treachery and deception.

Scholars also point to similarities between *Incidents* and Harriet Beecher Stowe's *Uncle Tom's Cabin, or Life Among the Lowly* (1852), which dramatized the plight of slaves and had such an impact on its readers that it is sometimes cited as one of the causes of the American Civil War. But although Stowe's "Uncle Tom" escaped only by dying, Linda's escape leads to a full life as a free woman.

Although Jacobs used the style of the 19th century romance in writing her narrative, presumably because it was the only model available to her, the content of her narrative focuses on her own experiences, and not—as was once believed—on the experiences of a fictional protagonist.

In conducting her research, Yellin also discovered a narrative written by Jacobs' brother, John. Titled *A True Tale*, the narrative authenticates Jacobs' experiences and provides a male perspective on many of the events described in *Incidents*.

Key Themes

Key themes in *Incidents* include the economics of slavery (see the Critical Essay "The Feminist Perspective"); the quest for freedom; pain and suffering (physical and emotional); self-definition; self-assertion; community support and family loyalty (generally lacking in slave narratives by men); and writing as a means of freedom, self-expression, and resistance. Also significant is the issue of literacy, which was often used as a metaphor for freedom, because slaves who learned to read and write were often the ones who ran away. Note, for example, that the letters Linda writes while hiding in her grandmother's garret play an important part in her eventual escape.

Other themes include the moral conflict between slavery and Christianity, color prejudice and racism, the bond of motherhood, family loyalty, and abandonment.

Narrative Structure and Chronology

As the Synopsis notes, *Incidents* can be divided into five distinctive parts each focusing on significant events in Linda's life.

Consequently, the structure deviates from that of the traditional slave narrative: Although some chapters focus strictly on Linda's story, others provide social, political, or historical commentary. The work also offers a new perspective on historical events such as the Nat Turner insurrection.

Incidents is unique in that it addresses a specific audience—white women in the North—and speaks for black women still held in bondage.

List of Characters

Linda Brent Pseudonym for the author, Harriet Ann Jacobs. Linda is born a slave in North Carolina. She eventually escapes to the North after spending 27 years in slavery, including the seven years she spends hiding in her grandmother's attic.

Aunt Martha Pseudonym for Molly Horniblow, Jacobs' grandmother. Aunt Martha, Linda's grandmother, is a free woman who provides Linda with love, support, and spiritual guidance. A former slave, Aunt Martha starts her own bakery business in order to earn enough money to buy her two sons, Benjamin and Phillip. After saving $300, she lends the money to her mistress, who never repays her. As a result, Aunt Martha is forced to live with the knowledge that although she is free, her family remains enslaved.

Miss Fanny A white woman who grew up with Aunt Martha in the Flint household. Angry at Dr. Flint for attempting to sell Aunt Martha, who has served his family for over 20 years, Miss Fanny buys her for $50, then sets her free.

William Possibly a pseudonym for Jacobs' actual brother, John. William is Linda's younger brother. He protects Linda and actively supports her quest for freedom.

Ellen and Benny Pseudonyms for Louisa Matilda Jacobs and Joseph Jacobs, the author's children. Ellen and Benny are Linda's two children by her white lover, Mr. Sands.

Dr. Flint Pseudonym for Dr. James Norcom, Jacobs' master and tormentor. Obsessed with Linda, Dr. Flint relentlessly pursues her, forcing her to make some drastic decisions to avoid his physical and sexual control.

Mrs. Flint Pseudonym for Mary Matilda Horniblow Norcom. The wife of Dr. Flint, Mrs. Flint recognizes her husband's sexual pursuit of Linda, and she becomes increasingly more abusive toward her.

Emily Flint Daughter of Dr. and Mrs. Flint. When Linda's mistress dies, Linda (age 12) is given to Emily, who is five years old at the time.

Mr. and Mrs. Flint Dr. Flint's son and daughter-in-law. When Linda refuses to succumb to Dr. Flint's sexual advances, he sends her to work on his son's plantation, where her first assignment is to prepare the house for the arrival of the new Mrs. Flint.

Mr. Sands Pseudonym for Samuel Tredwell Sawyer, the white man who fathers Linda's two children.

Betty The "faithful old friend" who helps Linda hide at the home of her mistress.

Jenny The slave who threatens to betray Linda's hiding place in the house of her mistress. As a result, Linda is forced to hide in her grandmother's attic.

Peter The friend who helps Linda during her first escape attempt.

Mrs. Durham The white woman who befriends Linda in Philadelphia and hires her as a nurse to her child.

Mrs. Bruce (First) Pseudonym for Mary Stace Willis, first wife of Nathaniel Parker Willis, who befriends Linda in New York. Mrs. Bruce, an English woman who abhors slavery, employs Linda as a nurse for her daughter, Mary. She also works to protect Linda from Dr. Flint.

Mrs. Bruce (Second) Pseudonym for Cornelia Grinnell Willis, Nathaniel Parker Willis' second wife. The second Mrs. Bruce is an American who also abhors slavery. On two occasions when Linda goes into hiding, Mrs. Bruce entrusts her to take her own infant daughter with her, knowing that if Linda is caught, the baby will be returned to her, and she will be informed of Linda's whereabouts. The second Mrs. Bruce finally buys Linda's freedom for $300.

Character Map

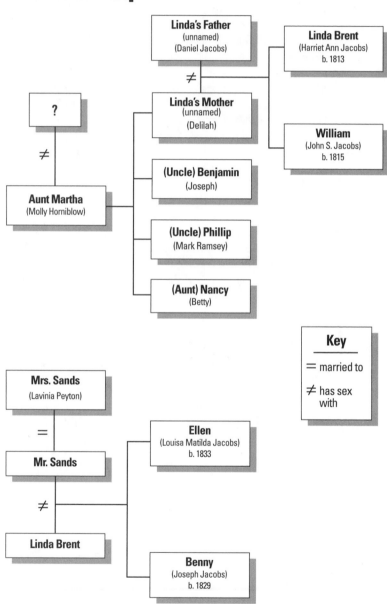

Linda's Father
(unnamed)
(Daniel Jacobs)

Linda Brent
(Harriet Ann Jacobs)
b. 1813

≠

Linda's Mother
(unnamed)
(Delilah)

?

≠

Aunt Martha
(Molly Horniblow)

William
(John S. Jacobs)
b. 1815

(Uncle) Benjamin
(Joseph)

(Uncle) Phillip
(Mark Ramsey)

(Aunt) Nancy
(Betty)

Key

= married to

≠ has sex with

Mrs. Sands
(Lavinia Peyton)

=

Mr. Sands

≠

Linda Brent

Ellen
(Louisa Matilda Jacobs)
b. 1833

Benny
(Joseph Jacobs)
b. 1829

CRITICAL COMMENTARIES

Chapter 1

Summary

As the narrative opens, Linda Brent recounts the "unusually fortunate circumstances" of her early childhood before she realized she was a slave. Linda's father is a carpenter who—because of his extraordinary skills—is granted many of the privileges of a free man. The chapter introduces Linda's mother, her brother William, and her Uncle Benjamin, who is sold at age ten. Linda also introduces her maternal grandmother (referred to as Aunt Martha by the white community), a strong-willed, resourceful woman who establishes a bakery to earn money to buy her children's freedom. She manages to earn $300, which she loans to her mistress, who never repays her.

When Linda is six years old, her mother dies. When she is 12, her mistress dies, and Linda is sold to the five-year-old daughter of her mistress' sister.

Commentary

Style & Language

Like many other formerly enslaved black men and women who documented their life stories, such as Frederick Douglass and Mary Prince, Brent opens her narrative with the statement, "I was born." This phrase is not followed, as readers might expect, by the date and place of her birth, but by the words "a slave." Consequently, as the Introduction notes, Brent's narrative, supplemented by the obligatory advocacy letters and testimonials, meets one of the primary conventions of the traditional slave narrative.

The connotation of these three words, which may seem imminently appropriate for the beginning of an autobiography, help readers recognize the power of personal narrative: Through their writings, which document their triumphant journeys from bondage to freedom, these men and women were, in fact, recreating themselves by rejecting their status as "property" and—through the process of a metaphorical "rebirth"—viewing themselves as unique human beings with the power to influence their own destinies.

Character Insight

Brent points out that she remained blissfully unaware of her enslaved status until the age of six, when her mother dies. Thus, she establishes within the first few pages of her narrative the powerful bond she shared with her mother. In subsequent chapters, readers discover that this maternal bond extends to the nurturing, supportive relationship she shares with her grandmother. Readers can also surmise that Linda's fierce, protective love for her children stems from the unconditional love she herself experienced as a child.

After establishing that black mothers are just as devoted to their children as their white counterparts, Brent relates the story of her grandmother, who was forced to watch her youngest son, Benjamin, sold at the age of ten. But despite her grandmother's circumstances, Brent does not portray her as a weak woman who passively accepts her fate. Instead, she describes her as a strong-willed woman determined to do everything in her power to keep her family together. Consequently, when she lends her mistress her hard-earned $300—which she had saved toward the purchase of her children's freedom—readers can identify with her pain and devastation upon realizing that her mistress has betrayed her trust. In short, Brent portrays her grandmother not as a helpless victim, but as a strong, albeit vulnerable, woman who has been exploited and victimized.

After her mother's death, Linda spends the next six years as the slave of her mother's mistress, who treats her well and keeps her promise to Linda's mother to care for her children. But when her mistress dies and Linda becomes the property of a five-year-old, she realizes that she is completely at the mercy of her "masters," and that, regardless of the kind treatment she has received, she is a slave.

Glossary

Here and in the following chapters, difficult words and phrases, as well as allusions and historical references are explained.

mulattoes 1. persons who have one black parent and one white parent. 2. technically, any persons with mixed black and white ancestry.

dower that part of a man's property which his widow inherits for life.

chattel 1. a movable item of personal property, as a piece of furniture, an automobile, or a head of livestock (in full *chattel personal*) 2. [Archaic] a slave.

Chapter 2

Summary

Dr. Flint, a neighborhood physician, had married the sister of Linda Brent's mistress, and Linda is now the property of their young daughter. The family also purchased her brother, William. The chapter opens with an incident concerning William, who is severely reprimanded by his father for answering to his mistress instead of his father after being summoned by both of them. Linda then recounts her friend's funeral, her father's sudden, unexpected death, and the sale of her grandmother.

Her grandmother's mistress had always promised that, upon her death, the grandmother would be granted her freedom. But when the mistress dies, Dr. Flint reneges on this promise and puts Linda's grandmother up for sale. However, the sister of the deceased mistress purchases her, and, finally, her grandmother is granted her freedom.

This chapter details vivid accounts of the Flints' cruelty and brutality—as well as that of neighboring slaveholders—toward their slaves.

Commentary

Character Insight

One of the most significant incidents in this chapter is the opening scene in which William learns "his first lesson of obedience to a master." Given Linda's description of her father's independent nature, his sudden, unexplained death may not have been an accident. This chapter offers a glimpse of Linda's naiveté concerning the brutality and violence often inflicted upon slaves when she remarks that she found it difficult to believe that her father was dead, because she hadn't even known that he was sick. The fact that she learns about her father's death at her friend's funeral compounds her loss, and she finds little comfort in her grandmother's consoling words.

Another key incident concerns the story of the silver candelabra purchased with the money Linda's grandmother had lent her mistress. Linda's remark that the candelabra will probably be handed down from generation to generation underscores the fact that Linda's family has been denied a family legacy. This issue is compounded when Dr. Flint not only refuses to repay Linda's grandmother, but he sells her instead of the candelabra for a mere $50.

The rest of the chapter illustrates the cruelties of Dr. and Mrs. Flint who, as their name implies, are cold, hard-hearted people. The closing scenes highlight the plight of female slaves who are forced to satisfy the lust of their lascivious masters. The author focuses on the story of a male slave who is nearly beaten to death for quarrelling with his wife because the master is the father of her children and the account of a slave girl who dies in childbirth soon after her baby dies.

Glossary

festoons wreaths or garlands of flowers, leaves, paper, and so on hanging in a loop or curve.

linsey-woolsey a coarse cloth made of linen and wool or cotton and wool.

epicure a person who enjoys and has a discriminating taste for fine foods and drinks.

joist any of the parallel planks or beams that hold up the planks of a floor or the laths (strips of wood used as a foundation for plaster) of a ceiling.

overseer one who watches over and directs the work of others; supervisor; here a person who supervised the work of slaves on a plantation.

incarnate endowed with a body, especially a human body; in bodily form.

Chapters 3 and 4

Summary

Linda compares the slaves' New Year's Day with the New Year's festivities enjoyed by whites. She notes that, for slaves, January 1 was hiring day. Thus, slaves were expected to leave their families behind and leave the plantation with their new masters on January 2. To illustrate the anguish this day brings to her people, Linda describes a scene of a mother standing by helplessly as all seven of her children are sold, and she tells about an owner who offers to sell an old woman who has served the family for 70 years to anyone who will give $20.

In Chapter 4, Linda tells the story of her Uncle Benjamin, her grandmother's youngest son, who runs away after striking his master. He is caught, imprisoned, and sold, but escapes again. After being briefly reunited with his brother, Phillip, he escapes to New York, where he passes as white. His mother finally manages to buy Phil's freedom, but Benjamin is lost to his family forever.

Commentary

In Chapter 3, Linda illustrates the "peculiar sorrows" of the slave mother. The scenes she describes of children being wrenched from their mothers' arms and sold to new "masters" must have a powerful impact on her, because—when she becomes a mother—she does everything in her power to save her children from a similar fate.

Linda's account of her Uncle Benjamin's escape by "passing" for white raises an important issue in the narrative, because light-skinned blacks often took advantage of "passing" to gain access to jobs and other opportunities they would otherwise be denied. Those who chose this path were, like Benjamin, often forced to sever all ties with friends and families for fear of having the secret exposed, although some were able to pass back and forth over the color line with relative ease.

Chapters 5 and 6

Summary

In Chapters 5 and 6, Linda, age 15, describes the daily torments she must endure in the Flint household. Pursued by the lecherous Dr. Flint, age 55, she invokes the jealous rage of Mrs. Flint who, instead of trying to protect Linda, sees her as responsible for arousing her husband's lust. To illustrate that her plight is no different from that of countless other black women, Linda tells the story of two sisters who are raised together even though one is the others' slave. But although the white girl grows up and gets married, her darker-skinned sister is left behind to endure the shame and degradation of sexual exploitation by her master.

When Dr. Flint realizes that he cannot coerce Linda into submitting to his advances with threats of violence or promises of favorable treatment, he comes up with a new scheme: He decides to bring his four-year-old daughter to his apartment and designates Linda as the child's servant, which requires her to sleep in the little girl's room at night. He then brings his daughter into his own bedroom, which requires Linda to sleep in his room.

When Mrs. Flint hears of this arrangement, she is furious and demands that Linda swear on her Bible that she did not sleep with her husband. Linda readily does so, and Mrs. Flint, temporarily satisfied, promises to protect Linda from her husband. Consequently, she demands that Linda sleep in a room adjoining her own, where she keeps a constant watch over her, an arrangement Linda eventually finds even more nerve-wracking than being pursued by Dr. Flint. When this new arrangement no longer satisfies her, she begins accusing her husband of improper behavior in front of Linda. When Linda realizes that the immature, emotional Mrs. Flint is totally at the mercy of her manipulative husband, she knows that she cannot count on her for protection.

Suspicious of the goings-on in the Flint household, Linda's grandmother offers to buy Linda's freedom, but Dr. Flint refuses, insisting that because Linda is the "property" of his daughter, he has no right to sell her.

Meanwhile, Dr. Flint continues to pursue Linda, alternating his threats of violence with promises of favorable treatment and appeals to Linda's "ingratitude" for not appreciating his "kindness."

Commentary

Character Insight

In these two chapters, Linda graphically depicts her situation as a young female slave caught between her lustful, manipulative master and his emotionally immature and insecure wife. She points out that although for white women beauty is a virtue, for black women, it is a curse that makes them more likely to become the objects of their masters' lusts. Although Linda realizes that she is a slave, she also acknowledges that she is a woman capable of arousing her mistresses' hate and jealously. Consequently, she is trapped in a dangerous situation over which she has no control. She despises Dr. Flint and realizes that the only person she can turn to for help is Mrs. Flint. But when she discovers that Mrs. Flint blames her for her husband's behavior, she knows that she must find some other way to escape Dr. Flint's relentless pursuit.

Theme

In Chapter 6, Linda reflects on the intricate relationships between black and white women and between white men and white women. In essence, she points out that both black and white women are at the mercy of the white patriarchal system that enables white men to exercise complete control over their wives, who—afraid that confronting their husbands' sexual misconduct will endanger their marriages—generally choose to ignore it and vent their wrath on their female slaves.

For example, in Chapter 6, Linda notes that a slave "is not allowed to have any pride of character." Several pages later, she admits that she "pitied Mrs. Flint" because "she was completely foiled [by her husband] and knew not how to proceed." She realizes that Dr. Flint does not allow his wife "to have any pride of character," because he does nothing to allay her suspicions, nor does he stop pursuing Linda even when his wife is fully aware of the situation. Because Mrs. Flint has no control over her husband's behavior, she turns her wrath on Linda, even though she realizes that Linda, like herself, is totally powerless to change the situation.

Linda points out that white women are both victims of and accomplices in their husbands' sexual exploitation of enslaved black women. She does acknowledge that the few women who do speak up often shame their husbands into freeing their slave children and that these women often "commanded their [husbands'] respect." But she points out that, in general, white women—whether they are Southerners steeped in the plantation tradition or Northerners enamored with the prospect of marrying a wealthy Southern landowner—are just as responsible as white men for perpetuating the institution of slavery.

Glossary

Yoke a wooden frame or bar with loops or bows at either end, fitted around the necks of a pair of oxen, etc. for harnessing them together; any mark or symbol of bondage or servitude.

piazza [New England and Southern U.S.] a large, covered porch.

perfidy the deliberate breaking of faith; betrayal of trust; treachery.

hoary-headed miscreant white-haired (old) troublemaker.

the Inquisition 1. *a)* a former general tribunal established in the 13th century for the discovery and suppression of heresy and the punishment of heretics. *b)* the activities of this tribunal. 2. *a)* any harsh or arbitrary suppression or punishment of dissidents or nonconformists. *b)* any severe or intensive questioning.

Chapter 7

Summary

Linda falls in love with a free black man who wants to marry her and offers to buy her, but Dr. Flint refuses to sell her. Fearing for her lover's life, Linda begs him to go to the Free States. Left alone, she is grateful for the company of her grandmother and her brother, William.

Commentary

Literary Device

This chapter foreshadows Linda's decision to embark on the "perilous journey" she describes in Chapter 10. It also offers insight into the true status of free blacks who—although free from slavery—were not free to enjoy the inalienable rights of white citizens. Free blacks were required to carry a certificate at all times. If they were caught without it, they risked being kidnapped and sold back into slavery. Even in Free States, blacks were not allowed to vote or to hold public office. They could not testify in court against whites, and they could not carry weapons, ride on buses and trains, or use public facilities designated as "White Only." If they failed to pay their debts or taxes, they were at risk of being enslaved. As more blacks gained their freedom, new laws were passed to restrict their hard-won rights. Even so, Linda's brief relationship with a free man strengthens her resolve to free herself from Dr. Flint's control.

Glossary

peeled and pickled [Informal or Slang] whipped and washed in brine.

ardor emotional warmth; passion.

forbearance 1. the act of forbearing, or controlling oneself under provocation. 2. the quality of being forbearing; self-control; patient restraint.

mortify to cause to feel shame, humiliation, chagrin, etc.

loquacious very talkative; fond of talking.

imprecations curses.

Free States states in which slavery was not permitted.

defray to pay or furnish the money for (the cost or expenses).

Chapters 8 and 9

Summary

In Chapters 8 and 9, Linda digresses from her personal narrative to address some broader issues concerning the conditions of slaves and the institution of slavery. In these two chapters, she focuses on the reasons that many slaves didn't defy the slaveholders or attempt escape.

In Chapter 8, Linda discusses the lies and misinformation (about the Free States) that slaveholders communicated to slaves in order to discourage them from running away. For example, one slaveholder shares a story about a runaway facing death from starvation. She also holds Northerners accountable for their complicity in slavery, especially for enforcing the Fugitive Slave Law.

Briefly in Chapter 8 and throughout Chapter 9, Linda describes the physical violence inflicted on slaves by slaveholders. Linda presents harrowing tales concerning the murder, torture, and abuse of slaves on plantations owned by three neighboring slaveholders: Mr. Litch, Mr. Conant, and Mrs. Wade.

Commentary

Chapters 8 and 9 focus on the methods slaveholders use to instill fear in their slaves. Slaveholders impart lies about the Free States and the possibilities of freedom. Linda stresses that the majority of slaves are deliberately kept in ignorance about the North. Despite the brutal treatment some slaves are subjected to at the hands of their masters, they are taught that they cannot survive on their own and are better off where they are. Slaveholders subject their slaves to acts of extreme violence. Because of this brutality, slaves fear the consequences of fleeing or defying their masters. And many slaves are too physically and/or emotionally broken to risk an escape into the unknown.

Theme

Linda believes that knowledge is the key to gaining freedom from the bonds of slavery—an important theme throughout the book.

Many slaves believe the slaveholders' lies about the futility of running away—the "deplorable" conditions, starvation, and so on.

However, Linda explains that slaves with more accurate information are aware that some people in the Free States are willing to help them and, thus, a better quality of life is possible. Linda says that with teaching, slaves can "begin to understand their own capabilities, and exert themselves to become men and women."

Although Linda applauds both knowledge and defiance, she knows that a slave isn't accountable for his brutalized condition. The cause, she says, "is the ignorance in which white men compel him to live; it is the torturing whip that lashes the manhood out of him; it is the fierce bloodhounds of the South, and the scarcely less cruel human bloodhounds of the north. . . ."

Although Linda herself is not subjected to the brutal physical abuse that Chapter 9 describes, she is forced to endure extreme mental and psychological anguish as she fights to free herself from Dr. Flint. Her own education—for example, her ability to read newspapers—provides her with a look at the possibilities of freedom in the North.

Glossary

veracity accordance with truth; accuracy of statement; that which is true; truth.

Fugitive Slave Law This law, passed in 1850, dictated that even slaves who had reached sanctuary in the Free States were subject to the possibility of being returned to slavery. Linda discusses the impact of this law in Chapter 40.

bloodhounds any of a breed of large dogs with a smooth coat, wrinkled face, drooping ears, and a keen sense of smell; bloodhounds are used in tracking escaped prisoners, fugitives, etc. Bloodhounds were often trained to track and sometimes kill runaway slaves.

the peculiar institution a euphemism for the institution of slavery.

abolitionists people who fought to end slavery.

The eighth commandment "Thou shalt not steal."

depredations acts or instances of robbing, plundering, or laying waste.

freshet a stream or rush of fresh water flowing into the sea.

Prostrate lying flat, prone (face downward), or supine (face upward).

mortifying [Now Rare] causing (body tissue) to decay or become gangrenous.

cotton gin a machine for separating cotton fibers from the seeds.

manumit to free from slavery; liberate (a slave, serf, etc.).

licentiousness moral unrestraint, esp. in sexual activity; lasciviousness.

profligate immoral and shameless.

vitiated morally weakened; debased; perverted.

Chapters 10 and 11

Summary

In Chapter 10, Linda resumes her story from Chapter 7 about her relationship with the free black carpenter. Having refused the man's offer to buy Linda's freedom, Dr. Flint adopts a new tactic to try to win Linda's submission: He offers to build her a house and make her "a lady." In desperation, Linda decides to enter into a sexual relationship with Mr. Sands, a white lawyer who has shown an interest in her. Reasoning that he is unmarried, that he seems to be a gentleman, and that—if she consents to be his mistress—he will most likely buy her from Dr. Flint, Linda consents to his advances and becomes pregnant by him. The next time Dr. Flint approaches her, she experiences a moment of triumph when she tells him that she is carrying another man's child.

When she tries to explain her situation to her grandmother, she finds it difficult to speak. Consequently, her grandmother, thinking that Linda has given in to Dr. Flint, turns her out of her house. Heartbroken at the thought that she has disgraced her family, Linda leaves in tears and finds shelter at a friend's home. After confessing her situation, the friend convinces her to send for her grandmother and tell her the truth. Linda does so, and the two women reconcile.

Linda returns home to live with her grandmother. Concerned for her welfare, Linda's grandmother speaks to Mr. Sands, who promises to care for Linda and her child.

Meanwhile, Dr. Flint is outraged at what he perceives as Linda's betrayal and tries to coerce her into revealing her lover's identity. When she refuses, he reaffirms his vow that she will remain his slave for life.

Shortly before Linda's baby is born, her Uncle Phillip comes for a visit. Linda is ashamed of her condition and, at first, tries to avoid him. But she finally agrees to see him and is touched by his compassion.

Linda is exhausted from physical and emotional stress, and she becomes critically ill, but refuses to let Dr. Flint treat her. Her baby is born prematurely and both mother and child are weak and sickly for a year, during which Dr. Flint visits them on occasion, meanwhile venting his wrath on Linda's brother, William, who works as his assistant. Gradually, Linda and her baby boy—who remains nameless—regain their strength.

Commentary

Much like the Africans who were forced onto slave ships to begin their perilous passage across the Atlantic, Linda—by choosing to enter into a sexual relationship with Mr. Sands—embarks on a perilous passage from which there is no turning back. Although she regrets the pain she is causing her grandmother, she does not try to rationalize or justify her decision, but openly admits that, given her intolerable circumstances, she sees no other way out.

Linda claims accountability for her actions and expresses intense guilt and shame for what she has done: "My self-respect was gone! I had resolved that I would be virtuous, though I was a slave." However, she acknowledges, understands, and tries to communicate her powerlessness: "I feel that the slave woman ought not to be judged by the same standard as others." Like many women throughout history, Linda was judged by a moral standard that she wasn't allowed the personal power to adhere to.

Linda's relationship with her newborn son is a major turning point in her life. As she contemplates her son's dismal future, her emotions run the gamut from fierce, protective love to overwhelming fear at the thought of having her son torn from her arms and sold to another master.

Black people, both slaves and free, were often powerless to help and protect loved ones, and the pain this helplessness caused is the underlying theme of Chapter 11.

For example, Linda's grandmother is concerned about Linda and the baby, and she speaks with Mr. Sands (the child's father), chastising him and imploring him to care for Linda and his child. He agrees to care for the child and to try to buy Linda. However, Dr. Flint avows that he will never sell her. So both Linda's grandmother and Mr. Sands are powerless to protect her from Dr. Flint.

Linda's brother, William, works as Dr. Flint's assistant, and he is often forced to watch his master threaten and humiliate Linda. When he shows tears brought on by his frustration at being unable to help her, Dr. Flint puts him in jail.

The chapter ends with Linda's frantic concern over her child's illness and her inability to heal him. Linda has seemingly conflicting emotions about her son. Although she loves him dearly, she finds herself wishing him dead to keep him from being subjected to a life of slavery. According to scholars and historians familiar with this era, such feelings were not unusual among slave mothers.

Although Linda enjoys and is dedicated to her son, she must always carry the burden that her child is a slave, and she doesn't have the power to free him or protect him: ". . . always there was a dark cloud over my enjoyment. I could never forget that he was a slave."

Glossary

boon 1. [Archaic] a request or the favor requested. 2. a welcome benefit; blessing.

intimated [Archaic] made known formally; announced.

wormwood any of a number of strong-smelling plants (genus *Artemisia*) of the composite family, with white or yellow flowers; especially, a Eurasian perennial (*A. absinthium*) that yields a bitter, dark-green oil (wormwood oil) formerly used in making absinthe (a poisonous alcoholic drink having a flavor somewhat like that of licorice).

countenance 1. the look on a person's face that shows one's nature or feelings 2. the face; facial features; visage.

smote [Now Rare] hit or struck hard; defeated, punished, destroyed, or killed.

Chapters 12 and 13

Summary

Linda describes the aftermath of the Nat Turner rebellion and denounces the moral conflict between the doctrine of the Christian church, which teaches love and brotherhood, and the brutal and amoral behavior of men and women who profess to be Christians.

Commentary

In these two chapters, Linda again digresses from her personal narrative to address broader issues affecting the black community. In Chapter 12, she describes the aftermath of the Nat Turner insurrection. Lawless whites, with the permission of southern slaveholders, ransack slave cabins and terrorize black men, women, and children whom they perceive as potential rebels.

Theme

In Chapter 13, she exposes the hypocrisy of the Christian church. Religion and spirituality have always been important themes in black literature, much of which is rooted in sermons and spirituals. The Church's hypocrisy is exemplified by the Rev. Mr. Pike whose favorite text is "Servants, be obedient to them that are your masters according to the flesh, with fear and trembling, in singleness of your heart, as unto Christ" (Ephesians 6:5).

In contrast to Rev. Pike are the new minister and his wife, who establish a special sermon for blacks, teach their slaves to read and write, and eventually set them free. Linda cites her own experience of teaching an elderly black man to read the Bible, thus she illustrates the critical link between freedom and literacy and exposes the hypocrisy of Christian missionaries who travel abroad to spread the gospel to "heathens," but conduct themselves as "heathens" in their own country by enslaving and brutalizing their black brothers and sisters. To further emphasize the differences between the perception and reality of slavery, she describes the tactics slaveholders use to convince those sympathetic to enslaved blacks that slavery is basically a benign "patriarchal institution."

Linda also describes the differences between Christianity and religion, and between the white church and the black church. Emphasizing the inherent spirituality of blacks, whose beliefs are rooted in African tribal religions, she highlights the hypocrisy of whites who discount these religions and attempt to convert blacks to a religion that teaches them that they are inferior beings.

Glossary

insurrection a rising up against established authority; rebellion; revolt.

muster to assemble or summon (troops, etc.), as for inspection, roll call, or service.

scourge 1. to whip or flog 2. to punish, chastise, or afflict severely.

consternation great fear or shock that makes one feel helpless or bewildered.

malediction 1. a calling down of evil on someone; curse 2. evil talk about someone; slander.

wounded Samaritans This is a reference to the parable of the Good Samaritan (Luke 10:33).

a Methodist shout a lively church service marked by loud singing and call-and-response sermons (shouts).

Chapters 14 through 16

Summary

Linda bears another child, a daughter, and despite Dr. Flint's protests, both children are baptized. She names her son Benjamin, after her favorite uncle, and her daughter Ellen, after her father's mistress.

With two children to care for, Linda's life is even more challenging, because Dr. Flint begins to use her children to punish and control her. After again refusing to sell her and her children, Dr. Flint offers to buy their freedom if Linda will consent to live with him as his mistress. When she refuses, he threatens to send her and her children to live on his son's plantation. Linda finally succumbs to—as the lesser of two evils—go to the plantation.

Linda and Ellen leave for Mr. Flint's plantation. Ben is ill so Linda leaves him behind with her grandmother. At the plantation, Linda resolves to work hard, but adamantly resists being "broken in." Because her new duties—which include preparing the household for the arrival of the new Mrs. Flint—are extremely demanding, Linda is forced to leave Ellen on her own for most of the day. After a terrifying incident during which Ellen is nearly killed by a snake, Linda realizes that she can no longer care for her daughter and sends her back to live with her grandmother. When Mr. Flint objects, she tells him that Ellen is sick and he lets the incident pass.

Over the next several weeks, Linda, accompanied by a young man from the plantation, sneaks home several times to visit her children. During one of her visits, she reveals her plans to escape, but changes her mind when her grandmother reminds her that her first responsibility is to her children. But when she accidentally learns that Dr. Flint plans to send her children back to Mr. Flint's plantation, she renews her resolve and begins to plot her escape.

Commentary

In these three chapters, Linda focuses on the new hardships she is forced to endure as the mother of two young children. She is especially distraught at the birth of her daughter, because she realizes that, as a female, the child will be forced to follow in her footsteps: "When they told me my new-born babe was a girl, my heart was heavier than it had ever been before. Slavery is terrible for men; but it is far more terrible for women."

In Chapter 15, Linda is presented with a heart-rending dilemma: Dr. Flint offers to give her and her children freedom if Linda will consent to live as his mistress. He promises to procure her a cottage, where she can live with her children. She must make a pivotal decision, one of the most difficult that any mother could face. In order for her children to be free, she must accept sexual servitude to an emotionally and sometimes physically abusive man whom she despises. And such an arrangement violates Linda's devout Christian beliefs. (In Chapter 14, Linda takes a great risk by having her children baptized in the church. Because blacks were believed to be creatures without a soul, this ceremony was generally restricted to whites.)

Possibly the greatest burden of Linda's life is that her children are living in slavery. And now she is being offered the opportunity to see her children free if she sacrifices her own morality. Compared to the lives of other slaves, this living arrangement provided benefits. She would be able to live *with* her children, in relative privacy, and Dr. Flint promises that her work duties will be light.

Linda doesn't accept Dr. Flint's offer, choosing instead to go to the plantation. Dr. Flint threatens that her son will be put to work, and both of her children will ultimately be sold. Readers may question Linda's decision. But throughout her life, Linda has been betrayed by white people. Her understandable reluctance to trust in their promises is a recurring theme throughout the narrative. She knows that Dr. Flint would not fulfill his promises, and the legal documents he drew up would be invalid: "I knew that my master's offer was a snare, and that if I entered it escape would be impossible." So she believes that her decision to go to the plantation is "inevitable."

Glossary

reprobate an unprincipled or totally bad person.

vituperations abusive language.

paramour a lover or mistress; especially, the illicit sexual partner of a married man or woman.

Chapters 17 through 20

Summary

Linda escapes from Mr. Flint's plantation and heads for her grandmother's house, where she persuades Sally, "a faithful friend," to help her reach the home of another friend, who hides her in a closet. After hiding at her friend's home for a week, Linda's pursuers come into close vicinity. She flees, terrified of being discovered, and hides for two hours in some nearby bushes, where she is bitten by a poisonous reptile. In excruciating pain, she returns to her friend's house, where she is treated with homemade medicine.

Meanwhile, Linda has contacted some of her relatives, who advise her to return to her master, beg his forgiveness, and accept her punishment. But when her friend informs her family of the pain and suffering Linda has endured in her struggle to remain free, they stop trying to convince her to go back. Desperate to help Linda, her grandmother enlists the aid of a woman she has known since childhood, who offers to help her escape and agrees to let her stay at her home until she can get to the Free States. The woman arranges for her cook, Betty, to meet Linda at a designated place and bring her to her home. When Linda receives the message to meet "a friend" at a secret location, she is surprised to discover that the "friend" is Betty. Betty escorts her back to her mistresses' house, brings her supper, and shows her to her new hiding place: an old storage room.

Linda learns that Dr. Flint has had her brother, William, her children, and her aunt (who has served the Flint family for over 20 years) arrested, hoping to force them into revealing her hiding place. Devastated that her actions are causing her family so much suffering, Linda considers turning herself in, until she receives a note from her brother, begging her to stay put and convincing her that turning herself in now would only serve to further endanger her family.

After a month, Linda's aunt is released and her daughter, Ellen, is taken to Dr. Flint's home, where she is treated for the after-effects of measles. That night, Dr. Flint, on his way back from seeing a patient, passes by Aunt Martha's cabin. Noticing that her light is still on and suspecting that Linda might be hiding at her grandmother's, he stops by to tell her that he knows where Linda is and will have her back by 12:00. He hopes that she will reveal Linda's hiding place. Alarmed, Aunt Martha and Uncle Phillip send a message to Betty's mistress, and Betty conceals her under some planks beneath the kitchen floor.

Several days later, Dr. Flint comes to the house where Linda is hiding, and Linda once again fears that she has been discovered. But after he leaves, her friend tells her that Dr. Flint—who has already posted a reward notice of $300 for Linda's capture—came to borrow $500 so that he could search for her in New York. She assures Linda that she is safe and has nothing to fear.

When Dr. Flint returns from New York, Linda's friends trick him into selling William (her brother), Ben (her son), and Ellen (her daughter) to a slave trader who represents Mr. Sands. The trader pretends to leave town with them, but then releases William and the children and allows them to go back to Aunt Martha. Linda, who is unaware of these transactions, has a vision in which she sees her children. Terrified that her children are dead, she turns to Betty, who reassures her that they are safe at home with her grandmother.

Dr. Flint has Phillip arrested on charges of aiding Linda's escape and demands $500 bail for his release. Meanwhile, the hunt for Linda continues and Betty again hides her under the kitchen floor. Just as she begins to feel safe, Jenny, another household slave, threatens to reveal Linda's hiding place. Afraid that she will be discovered, Betty's mistress contacts Phillip, who arranges for a friend to meet her. Disguised as a sailor, Linda meets Phillip's friend, Peter, who escorts her to the wharf, where Aunt Nancy's husband smuggles her aboard a ship, providing her with a temporary shelter. Later, Peter takes her to hide in Snaky Swamp, where Linda is terrified of the huge snakes. Although she is able to spend the night aboard the docked ship, Linda is forced to spend another day hiding out in the swamp. The following morning, Peter tells her that a hiding place has been secured for her. Linda, who has become severely ill from her ordeal, dons her sailor's disguise, blackens her face with charcoal, and follows Peter back to her grandmother's house.

Commentary

Style & Language

Linda recounts the harrowing circumstances surrounding her first "flight" or escape. The motif of flight (which can refer to literal flight or escape) is prevalent in numerous works by African American authors, such as Walter White's *Flight*, Ralph Ellison's *Flying Home*, Ishmael Reed's *Flight to Canada*, and Toni Morrison's *Song of Solomon*, which is based on the myth of the flying Africans. The language of flight is common in Jacobs' narrative. For example, when she makes her initial escape, she heads toward her grandmother's house "with almost lightening speed." And as her pursuers near her hiding place in a friend's home, she says, "I flew out of the house, and concealed myself in a thicket of bushes."

Theme

Masks, disguises, and deceptions are another prominent theme throughout the narrative. For example, Linda's escape depends on her ability to trick Dr. Flint by writing him letters that her friends then postmark from New York. Note also that when Linda boards the ship, she is disguised as a sailor. Benjamin escapes by passing, or masking his true identity, and Linda's son later follows in his great-uncle's footsteps. Linda also focuses on the fact that slavery deprives people of their ability to trust others. And for enslaved blacks, masking one's true feelings and identity was often crucial for survival.

In addition to masks and disguises, snakes are another key symbol in these chapters. In Chapter 18, Linda is bitten by a poisonous reptile, probably a snake, while hiding in the bushes from her pursuers. And in Chapter 20, Linda hides in Snaky Swamp, where she and Peter are surrounded by "snake after snake crawling round us." Because snakes can shed their skin, they often symbolize rebirth or renewal. Recall, however, that in the biblical story of the Garden of Eden, a snake tempted Eve and as a result, Adam and Eve were evicted from the Garden. Therefore, snakes can symbolize both birth and death. Although Linda is terrified of snakes, she prefers hiding out in Snaky Swamp over returning to her master: "even those large, venomous snakes were less dreadful to my imagination than the white men in that community called civilized." Snaky Swamp symbolizes the death of her old life and the perilous beginnings of her new life as a fugitive.

Glossary

fetters shackles or chains for the feet.

tarpaulin waterproof material; specifically, canvas coated with a waterproofing compound.

Chapter 21

Summary

Linda hides out in her grandmother's garret (attic), a dark, cramped crawl space infested with rats, mice, and "little red insects." Able to see her children through a small opening in the wood but unable to communicate with them, she spends several miserable months suffering a myriad of ills, including fever and frostbite. Meanwhile, Dr. Flint tries to bribe her children into telling him about Linda's whereabouts.

Commentary

The title of this chapter is "The Loophole of Retreat." A "loophole" provides a means of escape from a seemingly impossible situation. For example, a criminal captured at the scene of a crime may be set free because the evidence used to indict him was obtained without a proper search warrant. Similarly, a shrewd business owner may avoid paying taxes because she understands the intricacies of tax loopholes. However, the meaning of the word "retreat" depends primarily on its context. For example, a writer's retreat may be a refuge or sanctuary where writers overwhelmed by the pressures and demands of everyday life can go to relax and nurture their creativity, whereas a military retreat connotes an image of soldiers fleeing from the battlefield to escape their enemies. Linda's "loophole of retreat" offers both escape and sanctuary. When describing the oppressive darkness of her "loophole," Linda concludes, "It seemed horrible . . . Yet I would have chosen this, rather than my lot as a slave".

Character Insight

Linda's daring escape invites comparison to the story of Henry "Box" Brown, who escaped slavery by having himself packed in a crate and shipped to a Free State. But although Henry spent only hours— or, at most, days—in his box, Linda spends seven years virtually buried alive. She survives her harrowing ordeal by first transforming her mind—continually reminding herself that although confined in a cramped attic, she is free from Dr. Flint—and then transforming her space from a virtual grave to a "retreat."

For enslaved Africans, freedom generally meant crossing the boundaries from Slave States to Free States. After the passage of the Fugitive Slave Act in 1850, it meant crossing the boundaries between the United States and Canada or Mexico. But it also meant crossing mental boundaries and escaping the plantation mentality created and perpetuated by slaveholders who brainwashed blacks to believe that their subservient status was ordained by God. Escape generally involved breaking out of a confined, limited space. But Linda's escape entails movement from a larger, limited space to a confined space where, although physically imprisoned, she feels psychologically free.

Linda's seclusion in her "small, dark enclosure" symbolizes the narrow role—restricted because of both race and gender—prescribed for black women by white America.

Linda's ordeal also addresses the themes of madness and confinement prevalent in women's literature, such as Charlotte Perkins Gilman's short story, "The Yellow Wallpaper," in which a woman goes mad as a result of being isolated from society by her controlling and overbearing husband. But unlike Gilman's protagonist, Linda staves off madness by sewing for her children and writing letters to Dr. Flint, which she has postmarked from New York, to confuse him as to her whereabouts. Her ability to write not only helps her maintain her sanity, but it enables her to transform and transcend her reality.

Glossary

garret the space, room, or rooms just below the roof of a house, especially a sloping roof; attic.

gimlet a small boring tool with a handle at right angles to a shaft having at the other end a spiral, pointed cutting edge.

Chapter 22

Summary

Linda describes the rituals and festivities surrounding Christmas, focusing on the Johnkannaus dancers. She discusses her grandmother's two "special" guests—the town constable and the "free colored man" who tries to pass for white—who are invited specifically to convince them that Linda is nowhere near her grandmother's house.

Commentary

As in Chapter 3, Linda focuses on the role of traditions and celebrations in the black community. Christmas is a joyous occasion for both races, although the black community's festivities are overshadowed by the knowledge that hiring day (the day when slaves were expected to leave their families and go with their new masters) is near. Despite this knowledge, the slaves do their best to create a festive atmosphere that focuses on the Johnkannaus dancers. The fact that enslaved blacks celebrate the festival indicates that they have retained some aspects of their cultural heritage, despite enslavement.

Linda's grandmother opens the house for the constable and a free black man, "who tried to pass himself off for white, and who was always ready to do any mean work for the sake of currying favor with white people." Linda's attitude toward these men reveals some of her values. Although she finds the duties of the white constable "despicable," she expresses profound revulsion for the free black man, ". . . for the sake of passing himself off for white, he was ready to kiss the slaveholders' feet. How I despised him!" Although many blacks tried to pass as white to ensure their own survival—including Linda's Uncle Benjamin—this free black man had turned on his own people, a betrayal that brings up strong emotions for Linda.

Glossary

Johnkannaus a West African fertility ritual associated with the yam harvest and revolving around a cast of colorfully-costumed dancers.

Chapters 23 through 25

Summary

Linda continues to hide in the garret, but when she learns that Mr. Sands has been elected to Congress and will leave for Washington shortly, she risks revealing her hiding place to beg him to free her children before he leaves. He agrees to do what he can.

After Mr. Sands leaves, Linda writes numerous letters to Dr. Flint and—with the help of her friends—has them postmarked from New York to trick Dr. Flint into thinking she has left the state.

Commentary

Linda's determination to trick or outwit Dr. Flint may bring to mind the experiences of Penelope, Odysseus' wife, who used her "cunning" to escape the pursuit of her numerous suitors. (Homer, *The Odyssey*, translated by Robert Fitzgerald. New York: Anchor Books, 1963. Book 2, 21–22.)

After assuring them that she would marry one of them only after she has finished weaving a shroud for Lord Laertes, she spends her days weaving the shroud and her nights unraveling it. Thus, like Penelope—whose husband, Odysseus, is generally cited as the ultimate trickster—Linda uses her cunning to save herself and her family.

Glossary

aperture an opening; hole; gap.

oakum loose, stringy hemp fiber gotten by taking apart old ropes and treated as with tar, used as a caulking material.

lineaments any of the features of the body, usually of the face, especially with regard to its outline.

Chapters 26 through 29

Summary

Linda receives several letters from her brother, William, who has gone to Washington with his master, Mr. Sands. Suddenly, the letters stop, and Linda learns that William has escaped. Initially, she fears for her children, thinking that Mr. Sands might decide to sell them to make up for his loss. But Mr. Sands—who feels confident that William will return—is more surprised and disappointed by William's action than angry. After overhearing her grandmother's conversation with an elderly woman whose children have all been sold, Linda reminds herself of William's resolve to be free and is finally able to rejoice in his freedom, although, like her grandmother, she fears for his safety.

Meanwhile, Mr. Sands makes plans to send Ellen to live with his sister in Illinois, while Benjamin is to live with Mr. Sands and his new wife. When Linda learns of the plans, she is devastated at the thought of not being able to see her children any longer, although she realizes that the moves would be in their best interests. Ultimately, Mr. Sands decides to send Ellen to live with some of his relatives in Brooklyn. On the eve of Ellen's departure, Linda comes out of hiding and spends the evening with Ellen.

Six months later, Linda's grandmother receives a letter announcing Ellen's safe arrival in Brooklyn.

About this same time, Aunt Nancy (Aunt Martha's twin sister) dies, and Linda's grandmother is devastated by her sister's death. Aunt Nancy's death also forces Linda to reexamine her situation and to renew her resolve to escape before she, too, dies as a slave. She also realizes that the longer she remains, the greater danger she poses for her grandmother, a fact that is brought home to her when she narrowly escapes being discovered by Jenny, the house slave of her former benefactress. With the help of Uncle Phillip and his friend Peter, plans are made for Linda and her friend Fanny to travel north. Before she leaves, Linda introduces herself to her son, Ben, whom she has not spoken to for seven years while she was in hiding. He confesses that he has known of her hiding place all along.

Commentary

One of the most striking incidents in Chapter 26 is Mr. Sands' refusal to accept that William has run away. Emphasizing his kindness toward William, whom he claims he treated like his own brother, Mr. Sands blames the abolitionists for luring William away and insists that he will return as soon as he discovers the harsh realities of life for free blacks. Although he has witnessed Dr. Flint's cruel treatment of William and the way other slaveholders treat their slaves, Mr. Sands, as a free white man, cannot truly comprehend the devastating, soul-destroying reality of slavery and considers his slaves to be the equivalent of indentured servants who will regain their freedom in time and at his convenience. As he points out, he had planned to give William his freedom in five more years, so he doesn't understand why he wants to run away.

From Mr. Sands' perspective, Williams' action constitutes a breach of trust and loyalty rather than a bold and daring strike for freedom. In this respect, Mr. Sands is not unlike Dr. Flint, who views Linda's refusal to submit to his advances in much the same way. Mr. Sands' professed ignorance of the brutal realities of slavery seems especially shallow and hypocritical given that he is fully aware that the mother of his two children has been reduced to living like a caged animal and he does nothing to help her.

Another key incident (in Chapter 27) is Aunt Nancy's death, which—coupled with Williams' escape, Mr. Sands' decision to send her children to the North, and Jenny's near discovery of her hiding place—is the impetus for Linda's decision to escape. She realizes the pain and futility of spending another seven years in her "retreat." She can no longer rationalize her suffering as the price she must pay to see her children, who are no longer there to soothe her soul. Witnessing her grandmother's inconsolable grief at the loss of her sister conjures up images of her own grief at the imminent death of her grandmother. She decides that she has no choice but to seize what may well be her last chance to escape.

Note that Linda credits her escape (Chapter 29) not to her own courage and daring—characteristics often emphasized in male slave narratives—but to the love and support of her Uncle Phillip, her friend Peter, and her grandmother. Also note that despite her own fear and inconsolable grief over leaving her beloved grandmother, Linda worries about Fanny's welfare and does what little she can to comfort her friend. Here again, Linda's actions underscore a recurrent theme in the book: the love and support of the black community, especially the community of women, as a critical component of the struggle for survival and freedom.

Glossary

factotum a person hired to do all sorts of work; handyman. Here, the term refers to a slave, not an employee.

Chapter 30

Summary

With the help of Peter and Phillip, Linda and Fanny are smuggled aboard a ship headed for Philadelphia. Although the ship's captain treats the women with kindness and respect, Linda is afraid to trust him, fearful that at any moment he might betray them and turn them in for a reward. Even though they are free, both women feel alone and abandoned, and mourn the loss of friends and family. Standing on the ship's deck, Linda and Fanny are both deeply moved when, for the first time in their lives, they see the sun rise over free soil.

Commentary

Character Insight

Although exhilarated by their hard-won freedom, Fanny and Linda are overwhelmed by feelings of loneliness, loss, and abandonment. However, Linda takes a first step toward trust. Initially, she fears that the captain and crew will betray them: "slavery had made me suspicious of every body." As the ship approaches Philadelphia, the captain realizes her concern and regrets that she doesn't trust him after such a long journey together. He assures Linda that he will see that they are protected until they depart. Linda admits to herself that this white man has acted honorably toward them and was worthy of their trust.

Glossary

spectre a ghost; apparition.

Anti-Slavery Society an organization dedicated to abolishing slavery.

verily [Archaic] in very (genuine or absolute) truth; truly.

Chapter 31

Summary

Upon arriving in Philadelphia, the ship's captain introduces Fanny and Linda to Rev. Jeremiah Durham, a kind man who invites Linda to stay with him and his wife, and finds a place for Fanny with one of his friends. After Linda spends five days with Rev. and Mrs. Durham, who treat her like family, she and Fanny continue their journey to New York. During this trip, Linda has her first taste of discrimination in the North when she learns that blacks are not allowed to ride in the first-class section of trains.

Commentary

Character Insight

Linda struggles to come to terms with the challenges of freedom and sheds her mental shackles. She has not yet fully internalized the fact that she is no longer a slave, having been thoroughly conditioned to respond as such. For example, in the middle of the night when the fire bells ring, Linda hurriedly dresses and prepares to help fight the fire, as she would have been expected to do when she was a slave.

When Mrs. Durham takes her to an artist's gallery and shows her the portraits of her children, Linda is struck by the beauty of the paintings, because she has never seen portraits of black people before. Her brief acquaintance with Rev. Durham's family and her visit to the gallery provide Linda with her first exposure to black middle-class life. Possibly, these experiences enable her to envision a better life for herself and her children and fuel her determination to secure her freedom.

Chapter 32

Summary

Linda reunites with her daughter Ellen, who has been living and working in New York with Mrs. Hobbs, a cousin of Mr. Sands. Overjoyed at seeing her daughter, Linda is dismayed to discover that Ellen has been neglected. Despite Mr. Sands' promise that Ellen would be sent to school, Linda finds that Ellen has not been given much of an opportunity to attend school, although she has lived with Mrs. Hobbs for two years. As Linda prepares to leave, Mrs. Hobbs tells her that Mr. Sands has given Ellen to her oldest daughter as her maid. Devastated that Mr. Sands has not kept his promise to free her children, Linda realizes that she will have no control over her children's future until she herself is legally free. Consequently, she writes to Dr. Flint and to his daughter to inquire about the terms of her sale. Dr. Flint responds that he will consider her request only if she returns to her rightful owners.

Commentary

Character Insight

Linda's comment concerning her preference for "a straightforward course" reveals her reluctance to resort to deceit and trickery to obtain her objectives, even though she knows that she has little or no choice in the matter. Her comment also reveals her moral conflict: As a Christian woman who has been instilled with a strict value system by her grandmother, she feels compelled to be honest and straightforward in her dealings with others, but as a slave who has been denied the right to make her own value judgments, she feels equally compelled to do whatever it takes to maintain her freedom. Thus, she finds herself in the painful position of having to compromise her morals in order to survive.

Enslaved men and women often had to resort to these tactics to ensure their own survival. And, historically, blacks were often stereotyped as sly and deceitful. Of course, the sly and deceitful tactics Dr. Flint uses to try to coerce Linda into submission make clear that the premise of such an illogical argument is rooted in racism.

Also significant is the incident with the hackman who attempts to exploit Fanny and Linda. Here again, Linda learns that freedom does not automatically lead to respect and dignity. However, she also realizes that she must learn to judge people by their actions rather than by their race, because several whites have stepped forward to help the two women.

Glossary

hackman the driver of a hack or carriage for hire.

Chapter 33

Summary

Linda searches for work, but finds job hunting difficult, because potential employers require recommendations that she, as a fugitive, is unable to provide. Finally she meets Mrs. Bruce, a kindly English woman, who hires her as a nurse for her baby, Mary. Mrs. Bruce is a "true and sympathizing friend" to Linda. When Linda is unable to perform her duties because constant stair climbing causes her legs to swell, Mrs. Bruce brings in her personal physician to attend to Linda. Mrs. Bruce also offers Linda the opportunity to bring Ellen to live with her, but Linda declines her offer for fear of offending Mrs. Hobbs. Mrs. Bruce also offers to have her personal physician, Dr. Elliot, attend to Ellen, who is still experiencing problems with her eyes, a condition related to a bout of measles at age two. But when Linda asks Mrs. Hobbs' permission for Ellen to see Dr. Elliot, she refuses. Later, she informs Linda that she has employed her own doctor to attend to Ellen. Meanwhile, Linda, who is using her meager earnings to help provide for Ellen, grows increasingly anxious about her daughter's future.

The chapter ends brightly, because William, Linda's brother arrives in New York—dressed in sailor attire—and reunites with Linda and Ellen. The three easily re-establish the bonds among them, "There are no bonds so strong as those which are formed by suffering together."

Commentary

A key incident in this chapter revolves around Ellen's working for the Hobbs family. Ironically, Linda's daughter is in the same situation that Linda herself was in when she worked for Dr. Flint's family. Although both women are now living in the North, their subservient social status remains virtually unchanged.

Theme

In this chapter, a recurrent theme of the book again emerges: Blacks of the slavery era were often powerless to come to the aid of loved ones who needed help. Linda's status as a fugitive prevents her from inviting Ellen to live with her, because making such an arrangement might offend Mrs. Hobbs. Linda again must feel the powerlessness of being unable to protect her children. However, at the end of the chapter, a second recurring theme is highlighted: The ease with which Linda, William, and Ellen re-establish their bonds shows the comfort and support that members of the black community provided to one another.

This chapter also clearly demonstrates Linda's continued and understandable reluctance to trust whites, even though she is now living in the North. But she regrets that she must continue to be wary, especially with Mrs. Bruce. "I longed for someone to confide in; but I had been so deceived by white people, that I had lost all confidence in them." However, Linda's improved circumstances are beginning to heal her emotionally; she enjoys the opportunities for reading and intelligent conversation, and she says, "I gradually became more energetic and more cheerful."

Glossary

pecuniary of or involving money.

politic having practical wisdom; prudent; shrewd; diplomatic.

Chapter 34

Summary

Linda receives a letter urging her to come "home," purportedly written by Emily Flint's brother. She recognizes the letter as being from Dr. Flint. She does not respond, and soon thereafter receives another letter from a friend, informing her of Dr. Flint's plans to visit the North. Determined to avoid him, Linda tells Mrs. Bruce she needs two weeks off to attend to urgent business in Boston.

Upon arriving in Boston, she writes to her grandmother and asks her to send her son, Ben, to Boston instead of New York. Several days later, she reunites with her son. Meanwhile, Linda learns that Dr. Flint is in New York looking for her. As soon as she hears that he has gone, she leaves Ben with her brother William and returns to New York.

Commentary

Even though Linda now lives in a Free State, Dr. Flint refuses to give up his relentless pursuit. Here again, letters play a major role in helping Linda maintain her freedom, as does her ability to "outfox" the fox. This chapter underscores the issues of deception and trickery raised in Chapter 25.

Glossary

subjoin to add (something) at the end of what has been stated; append.

fortnight [Chiefly British] a period of two weeks.

shoal a large group; mass; crowd.

sanguine cheerful and confident; optimistic; hopeful.

Chapter 35

Summary

Linda, as Mary's nurse, goes to Albany with Mr. and Mrs. Bruce aboard a steamboat. While on board, she is insulted by a black waiter who refuses to serve her. Upon returning to New York, Linda goes to Brooklyn to visit Ellen, whom she meets on her way to the grocery store. Ellen warns her not to go to Mrs. Hobbs' house, because Mrs. Hobbs' brother, Mr. Thorpe, is visiting from the South. Linda heeds her warning and tells Ellen that she will see her when she returns from her impending trip to Rockaway with the Bruce family.

Linda then recounts her experiences in a hotel in Rockaway, where she is refused the right to sit at the dining table with other, lighter-skinned black nurses, who shun her. At first, she relents and takes her meals in her room, but later, she refuses to accept their behavior and gradually wins their grudging respect.

Commentary

One of Linda's most painful realizations is that even though she now lives in a Free State, she is still subject to Jim Crow laws.

"Jim Crow" was a character introduced in 1832 by a song written and sung by "Daddy" Dan Rice in his minstrel act. Minstrel shows generally consisted of song-and-dance numbers by white performers in blackface makeup who portrayed blacks as clowns and buffoons. To racist whites, these caricatures of blacks reinforced their belief that blacks are innately inferior and, therefore, suited for the role of slave and servant. The term "Jim Crow" eventually became synonymous with "Negro," often spelled with a lowercase "n" to further emphasize the perceived inferiority of blacks.

In essence, Jim Crow laws aimed at keeping blacks "in their place" by legalizing discrimination. Numerous Jim Crow laws were in effect throughout the United States. These laws varied regionally, but they all enforced segregation (they kept the races separate). Jim Crow laws ensured that blacks and whites attended separate schools; traveled in separate railroad cars, streetcars, and taxicabs; used separate facilities such as parks, restrooms, and waiting rooms; and entered factories and other buildings through separate entrances. Spending for education was vastly unequal in favor of white children. And transportation, facilities, and other necessities designated for blacks were inferior compared to whites'.

This chapter makes clear, however, that Linda maintains her self-respect and will not respect the authority of discriminatory laws and customs. She successfully stands up for her rights, saying "Let every colored man and woman do this, and eventually we shall cease to be trampled under foot of our oppressors."

Glossary

Anglo-Saxon a member of the Germanic peoples (Angles, Saxons, and Jutes) that invaded England (5th-6th centuries A.D.) and were there at the time of the Norman Conquest.

Chapter 36

Summary

During a visit with Ellen, Linda learns that Mrs. Hobbs' brother, Mr. Thorpe, has written a letter to Dr. Flint, informing him of Linda's whereabouts and offering to help him regain his "property." Upon returning home, Linda tells Mrs. Bruce about her predicament and confesses that she is a fugitive slave. Mrs. Bruce immediately contacts her attorney, who helps arrange transportation to Boston for Linda, Ellen, and William, who has come to New York to escort his sister to safety. Upon their arrival in Boston, Ellen reunites with her brother, Ben. Linda decides to stay in Boston and share living expenses with a friend. She spends the winter helping Ellen learn to read and write so that she will be prepared to return to school.

Commentary

Theme

The key incident in this chapter focuses on the friendship between Linda and Mrs. Bruce, who trusts Linda with her own baby. Linda is finally able to count on someone outside of the black community.

Their relationship demonstrates the extension of the bonds of friendship among black women to include trustworthy white women.

Chapter 37

Summary

Linda is saddened to learn that Mrs. Bruce has died. When Mr. Bruce asks her to accompany him to England as Mary's nurse so that his daughter can visit her mother's relatives, she accepts. After arranging for her children's care, Linda goes to New York to meet Mr. Bruce and Mary, and they begin their voyage to England. After 12 days, they arrive in Liverpool and head to London, where, for the first time in her life, Linda is treated with respect and dignity and experiences "pure, unadulterated freedom." During her visit, Linda has an opportunity to compare the lifestyle of England's poor to that of the poor in the United States. As the houseguest of a clergyman and his family, she also gains a new perspective on Christianity and experiences the true meaning of love and grace. Although she had anticipated only a short visit, Linda remains in England for 10 months.

Commentary

Linda's observation of England's poor highlights the fundamental differences between poverty and slavery. It also underscores the fallacy that slavery was a "benign" institution that protected blacks and provided them with food and shelter in exchange for their labor. As Linda points out, even though England's poor have no material wealth, they have friends and families and are not subjected to the indignities of poor U.S. blacks, whose lives and families are destroyed by the chattel slavery system.

Chapter 38

Summary

Upon returning home to Boston, Linda learns that Ben has left on a whaling voyage to escape the abuse of his fellow apprentices, who have discovered that he is "colored." Heartbroken, Linda chides herself for having left her children alone for so long, but reminds herself that it was for the best.

Soon after her return, Linda receives a letter from Mrs. Dodge (formerly Emily Flint). In the letter, Emily comments on Linda's trip to England and invites her to come live with her and her new husband in Norfolk, Virginia. Although Linda is furious to discover that Dr. Flint and his family are still keeping track of her, she tells herself that as long as she stays in Boston, she is safe.

Commentary

In this chapter, Linda is forced to make some difficult decisions as she fights to keep her family together, including coming to terms with her son's decision to "pass" as a white man.

By attempting to appear white, Ben is following in the footsteps of his namesake, Linda's Uncle Benjamin, who became lost to his family. This causes Linda to experience the same anguish her grandmother did when her son decided to "pass."

Chapter 39

Summary

Linda has lived in Boston for two years, and her brother, William, offers to send Ellen to boarding school. Although she is reluctant to part with her daughter, Linda eventually agrees that this would be in her daughter's best interest. The night before Ellen is scheduled to leave, Linda tells her the truth about her father, Mr. Sands. To her surprise, she discovers that Ellen has known the truth all along.

Linda is lonely without her daughter, and gratefully accepts an assignment as a seamstress for a neighboring family. Upon returning home, she finds a letter from William, asking her to help him establish an anti-slavery reading room in Rochester. She agrees to work with him, but the project doesn't receive broad community support and fails. Linda spends the next year with the family of Isaac and Amy Post, well-known anti-slavery advocates whose Rochester, New York, home, was a well-known station on the Underground Railroad.

Commentary

Theme

After Linda tells Ellen the circumstances of her birth, Ellen confides that she was deeply hurt by the way her father favored his white child over her. But, again, readers see the recurring theme of the strength of the bonds within the black community; Ellen says to her mother, "But now I never think any thing about my father. All my love is for you." This chapter also clearly demonstrates that Linda is willing to make great sacrifice to ensure her daughter's advancement. Linda is dejected about her daughter's leaving, but although she must suffer another loss, she realizes the importance of the opportunity for Ellen to continue her education. Linda puts a high priority on knowledge as a means to personal power, and she has passed on this value to Ellen. Ellen hates to leave her mother alone, but knows that she must take the opportunity offered her: "I am almost sorry I am going, though I do want to improve myself."

Chapter 40

Summary

Disappointed by the failure of his business venture, William moves to California, taking Ben with him. Ellen continues to do well in school and when her teachers discover that she is the daughter of a fugitive slave, they do their best to protect her.

Alone and unemployed once more, Linda returns to New York and decides to visit Mary and Mr. Bruce. She learns that Mr. Bruce has remarried and he invites her to be the nurse for his new child. Aware of the recent passage of the Fugitive Slave Law, Linda hesitates, but then decides to accept his offer. The new Mrs. Bruce is an American woman but, like the former Mrs. Bruce, she treats Linda with kindness and respect.

As Linda considers the devastating consequences of the Fugitive Slave Law, she recalls that the law forced people who had lived in New York for as long as twenty years to uproot their families and escape to Canada. She specifically recalls the case of James Hamlin (Hamlet), said to be the first person arrested under the new law. She also tells a story about a slave named Luke and his cruel master, and Luke's eventual escape to Canada with his master's money.

Linda also learns that Dr. Flint is once more on her trail. Mrs. Bruce helps her escape to New England and entrusts her with her own baby. Linda seeks refuge in the country, where she remains for a month. When she learns that Dr. Flint has given up his pursuit, she returns to New York.

Commentary

The Fugitive Slave Law was an example of the type of legislation Southern whites instituted in a desperate effort to maintain their slave economy. The law caused great anguish and upheaval in the lives of blacks.

In this chapter, Linda demonstrates her commitment to knowledge and her continued bond with the black community. Every evening she examines the newspapers carefully to see which Southerners are in the vicinity looking for slaves. She does this for her own safety, but also "to give information to others, if necessary; for if many were 'running to and fro,' I resolved that 'knowledge should be increased.'"

Readers also see the continued development of Linda's strong political consciousness. She defends Luke, the slave who took his master's money and went to Canada: "I confess that I agree with poor, ignorant, much-abused Luke, in thinking that he had a *right* to that money, as a portion of his unpaid wages." She and William spend their last evening together talking about the passage of the Fugitive Slave Law, and she remarks at length about the North's hypocrisy in upholding such a law.

Glossary

iniquitous showing iniquity; wicked; unjust.

dissipation indulgence in pleasure to the point of harming oneself; intemperance; dissoluteness.

despotic of or like a despot, or tyrant; autocratic; tyrannical.

palsied afflicted with palsy, or paralysis of any voluntary muscle as a result of some disorder in the nervous system, which is sometimes accompanied with involuntary tremors.

cupidity strong desire, esp. for wealth; avarice; greed.

Linda had achieved mental and spiritual freedom, which enabled her to continue on despite incredible hardships and countless setbacks.

Thanks to her strong family roots and the positive examples of her uncles, brother, and grandmother, she saw herself as inherently worthy of freedom and refused to accept anything less. Consequently, she is a strong role model for today's black men and women, some of whom must face seemingly insurmountable hardships, as blacks struggle for full human and civil rights. Clearly, Linda Brent's courageous story entails lessons that are still relevant today.

Glossary

trepidation fearful uncertainty, anxiety, etc.; apprehension.

from pillar to post from one problem to another.

expostulations earnest reasoning with a person, objecting to that person's actions or intentions; remonstration.

antiquaries people who collect or study relics and ancient works of art.

CHARACTER ANALYSES

Linda Brent

As her unrelenting determination to free herself and her children indicates, Linda Brent is the epitome of the "strong black woman" who—against all odds—manages not only to survive but also to transcend seemingly insurmountable barriers. Although she does not exhibit exceptional physical strength, she does exhibit extraordinary psychological and spiritual strength, qualities that enables her to maintain her sanity during the seven years she spends hiding in her grandmother's attic. Linda is an intelligent, clear-thinking woman who willingly assumes responsibility for her choices. She is also extremely creative, as illustrated by her carefully crafted plan to elude Dr. Flint by writing him letters and having her friends mail them from New York and Philadelphia.

Linda's close relationships with her grandmother, brother, and uncles, and her friendships with Fanny and Mrs. Bruce show that she is a loving and compassionate person. Her initial empathy for Mrs. Flint, despite her mistress's jealousy and hatred toward her, illustrates that she is extremely empathetic. Linda is able to see beyond the barriers of race and class, and she recognizes that, as women, they share a common bond and are both the victims of a sexist, patriarchal society.

Having suffered numerous betrayals, Linda finds it difficult to trust people, but her distrust is gradually tempered by positive relationships, although she retains a cautious, guarded approach to life and an awareness that enables her to continue to elude her captors, even when she is finally "free."

Aunt Martha

Aunt Martha is the stabilizing force in Linda's life. She also models many of the qualities that enable Linda to escape her bondage. A free woman and entrepreneur, Aunt Martha starts a bakery to earn money to buy her children's freedom. As a devout Christian with strong religious principles of right and wrong grounded in the Bible, Aunt Martha finds it difficult to forgive Linda for her sexual liaison with Mr. Sands, although she eventually relents, offering kindness and compassion, if not forgiveness.

Readers can presume that Aunt Martha is an imposing woman, because Dr. Flint is afraid of her because she once chased a white man with a gun for insulting one of her daughters. Aunt Martha provides a nurturing, loving home for Linda. She encourages her to stand by her children and risks her own life to protect Linda and her children. Conversely, she also discourages Linda's initial plans for escape. Her continuous struggle to keep her family together suggests that she is torn between wanting to see her children free and wanting to keep them safe at home.

William

William does everything in his power to help Linda and her children. He is always there to support and comfort her. It is William who watches over Ben and Ellen when they are thrown into jail, and it is William who encourages Linda to escape. After William escapes from Mr. Sands, he remains in contact with Linda to let her know that he is safe, and when she herself escapes, he is there to look out for her and her family. When he is disappointed in his entrepreneurial venture to open a bookstore and reading room, William rebounds and continues his work with the abolitionists. Like his grandmother, he refuses to succumb to the negative elements of his environment.

Dr. Flint

Dr. Flint is a manipulative, amoral old man who enjoys wielding control over others. He has complete control over Linda, who is 40 years younger than he is, but this is not enough for him. He tries to force Linda to surrender mentally and emotionally to his domination. Although he does not beat or rape Linda, he constantly threatens her with violence and, as evidenced by his treatment of his other slaves, he has no qualms about inflicting vicious, brutal punishments. Having identified Linda as an "intelligent negro" who can read and spell, he singles her out for special treatment and derives more pleasure from abusing her mentally and emotionally than physically or sexually.

Having already fathered 11 slave children, he appears to have no regard for his wife, whom he manipulates as well as Linda. Although professing to be a Christian, his only concern is projecting a positive image in his community.

Mrs. Flint

Mrs. Flint, Dr. Flint's second wife, is much younger than her husband. She is naïve and insecure, and she lacks the emotional maturity to deal with her husband's lascivious behavior. Even though she realizes that Linda is a victim of her husband's lust, she turns her wrath on Linda rather than confront her husband, fearing that her pride and dignity are at stake. If she fully acknowledges the situation, she would have to be indignant at the idea of her husband desiring the sexual favors of a slave, when he has her to meet his needs. If she convinces herself that Linda is to blame, she can ignore her husband's behavior. Conversely, Mrs. Flint, a product of 19th century Victorian prudery, probably subscribes to the perception of white women as pure and virtuous, in contrast to black women, who are perceived as amoral creatures all too willing to indulge their masters' lust. Being unable to express her fear, Mrs. Flint seeks relief by venting her hatred and jealousy on Linda.

Uncle Benjamin

Because of their closeness in age, Linda thinks of Uncle Benjamin as more of a brother than an uncle. Therefore, his experiences touch her deeply, and Uncle Benjamin holds a special place in her heart, as illustrated by the fact that she names her son Ben.

Having been sold at age ten for $720, Benjamin also holds a special place in his mother's heart and she struggles diligently but unsuccessfully to buy her youngest son's freedom. In his 20s, Benjamin runs away, only to be captured, imprisoned, and eventually sold for $300. Determined to be free, he runs away again and, because of his light skin, is able to pass for white, although as a result of choosing this avenue of escape, he is lost to his family forever.

Benjamin's plight illustrates the soul-destroying experiences of a man forced to live as a slave. Linda's son also survives by passing as white, until his coworkers discover his true identity. Despite young Ben's family's struggles and sacrifices, his position in society is probably the same as that of his great uncle.

Mr. Sands

Compared to Dr. Flint, Mr. Sands appears to be a man who truly cares for Linda and does his best to protect her and her children.

Although Linda offers no details concerning their liaison, the text implies that Mr. Sands is kind to her and that he protects her from Dr. Flint. When Aunt Martha confronts him concerning his relationship with Linda, Mr. Sands promises to take care of her and her children. And when Dr. Flint imprisons Linda's children and her brother William, Mr. Sands arranges for their sale and for their safe return to Aunt Martha's. But although he promises Linda that he will free her children, he fails to keep his word. And even though he knows Linda is hiding in her grandmother's attic, subjected to the most horrendous living conditions, he does nothing to help her.

Unlike Dr. Flint, who shows little compassion for his wife, Mr. Sands shows some remorse for his behavior and tries to protect his wife from his sordid past. But although he has some redeeming qualities, Mr. Sands is part of the patriarchal system that perpetuates the enslavement of blacks and the sexual exploitation of black women. In short, although he does not abuse his slaves, he fits comfortably into his role as slave-master. Consequently, the characteristics that link the two men are stronger than those that set them apart.

The First Mrs. Bruce

Linda's friendship with the first Mrs. Bruce, an Englishwoman who abhors slavery, enables her to make the difficult adjustment to her new life in New York. Through her role as nurse to Mrs. Bruce's daughter, Mary, Linda begins to trust again and experiences a new kind of relationship with a white woman who, like herself, values her role as a mother and finds her freedom limited because of her gender.

Mrs. Bruce is also indirectly responsible for expanding Linda's horizons. After Mrs. Bruce's death, Linda travels to England with Mr. Bruce serving as Mary's nurse. This trip enables Linda to see the differences between the lifestyles of England's poor, who are rich in terms of friends and family, and America's slaves, who are denied even the right to maintain their families and care for their children.

The Second Mrs. Bruce

Linda's friendship with the second Mrs. Bruce is just as strong as, if not stronger than, her relationship with the first Mrs. Bruce. The second Mrs. Bruce is an American woman who, like her predecessor, abhors slavery, and she does everything she can to help Linda maintain her freedom from Dr. Flint. Even after Linda confesses that she is a fugitive, Mrs. Bruce risks her own safety and the safety of her infant daughter to help her. Ultimately, Mrs. Bruce purchases Linda's freedom, demonstrating not only her unconditional commitment to Linda's welfare, but also her dedication to the principle of freedom.

CRITICAL ESSAYS

The Slave Narrative Tradition in African American Literature

The slave narrative is a form of autobiography with a unique structure and distinctive themes that traces the narrator's path from slavery to freedom. Although traditional slave narratives such as Jacobs' *Incidents in the Life of a Slave Girl* and Frederick Douglass' *Narrative* exemplify these works, numerous contemporary black authors have adapted the slave narrative format.

Contemporary slave narratives (also referred to as neo-slave narratives) include works such as Richard Wright's *Black Boy* and *The Autobiography of Malcolm X*, co-authored by Malcolm X and Alex Haley. Both works trace the narrator's journey from poverty and mental slavery or imprisonment to freedom achieved primarily through an awareness of new choices and options, a determination to overcome societal and self-imposed limitations, and a willingness to assume personal responsibility for transforming one's life. Wright's "black boy"—much like the authors of traditional narratives—discovers a sense of freedom by writing, while Malcolm X transcends his role as hustler, pimp, and prison inmate to become a renowned spokesperson, leader, and political activist.

Toni Morrison's *Beloved* and Ernest Gaines' *The Autobiography of Miss Jane Pittman* exemplify the fictional slave narrative, a form that originated with works such as William Wells Brown's *Clotel: Or, The President's Daughter, A Narrative of Slave Life in the United States* (1853), the first novel by a black American; Harriet Wilson's *Our Nig: or, Sketches from the Life of a Free Black, in a Two-Story White House, North*, (1859), the first novel by a black woman in the United States; and Harriet Beecher Stowe's *Uncle Tom's Cabin* (1852), which used the fictional story of an elderly black man to focus attention on the horrors of slavery. Morrison's novel, *Beloved*, tells the story of Sethe, a woman who portrays a former slave who killed her daughter to save her from being returned to slavery. Gaines' work, written in the form of an interview with the fictional Miss Pittman, traces Miss Pittman's life from slavery to freedom as a Civil Rights activist.

Toni Morrison's *Song of Solomon* and Ernest Gaines' *A Lesson Before Dying* also incorporate elements of the slave narrative, but in these two works, both authors transform conventional elements to achieve new dimensions. For example, Macon "Milkman" Dead, the selfish, apathetic protagonist in *Song of Solomon*, achieves both mental and spiritual freedom only when he lets go of his materialistic lifestyle and returns to the South to reconnect with his cultural and historical roots. In *A Lesson Before Dying*, Jefferson, a young man on Death Row for a murder he did not commit, is able to cast off his slave mentality and free his mind and soul only when he learns to transcend society's perceptions of him as less than a man and begins to reconnect with his community and see himself as a human being entitled to respect and dignity.

Many critics applaud contemporary slave narratives because they show individuals rising from the depths of despair to overcome seemingly impossible odds. However, some critics contend that the narratives perpetuate the myth that people can overcome society's racism by sheer willpower and determination. Many critics believe that the narratives are deceptive because they offer a false sense of hope to blacks, while encouraging whites to think that if some blacks can break down barriers and cross over racial boundaries to achieve success, those who do not have only themselves to blame.

The Feminist Perspective

As Linda laments the birth of her daughter, Ellen, she says "Slavery is terrible for men; but it is far more terrible for women."

Why was slavery "far more terrible for women"? Because, as Jacobs' story so poignantly illustrates, in addition to the horrors and brutalities endured by enslaved men, women bore the added anguish of being wrenched from their children. To compound their pain and degradation, enslaved women were often used as "breeders," forced to bear children to add to their master's "stock," but denied the right to care for them. In fact, it was not unusual for the plantation master to satisfy his lust with his female slaves and force them to bear his offspring. As Linda points out, children from such unions were often sold to protect the honor and dignity of the slaveholder's wife, who would otherwise be forced to face the undeniable evidence of her husband's lust.

In describing the economics of slavery, historians point out that although male slaves were generally valued for their labor and physical strength, females were valued for their offspring.

When Jacobs wrote her narrative, she addressed the women of the North, hoping to make them aware that, unless they spoke out in protest, they were just as guilty as Southern slaveholders of supporting and perpetuating the system of slavery.

Although Jacobs' *Incidents* bears numerous similarities to Frederick Douglass' *Narrative*, in many ways, it is radically different because it addresses the issues of female bondage and sexual abuse from a woman's perspective. For example, although Douglass' story focuses on the quest for literacy and free speech, Jacobs' story focuses on the rights of women to protect their families and raise their children. And although Douglass' narrative revolves around the fight for freedom of one independent individual, Jacobs' describes the struggle for freedom of a woman supported by her family and community. In short, Jacobs presents a decidedly feminist view of slavery.

If readers compare the opening chapters of Jacobs' *Incidents* and Douglass' *Narrative*, they realize that Douglass expresses no emotional attachments to his mother and has no investment in his community. He watches his aunt being beaten and does nothing to try to help her, fearing his master's wrath will be turned on him. Even so, Douglass' narrative became renowned, and Douglass went on to become a famous orator and civil rights leader, while Jacobs' narrative was lost, and she slipped into virtual oblivion. Ultimately then, although both works trace the path from bondage to freedom, Jacobs' cause is personal (she wants to save her children), and Douglass' is, at least in part, political (he wants to be noted as a leader and activist).

This view is also apparent in the title of Jacobs' narrative. Unlike Douglass, who identifies himself as "an American Slave," Jacobs identifies herself as a slave *girl*, focusing on her female gender. Because she refers to herself as "a slave girl," she implies—and later states explicitly—that she is speaking not only for herself, but also for her sisters still in bondage. Also, Douglass focuses on his life, but Jacobs focuses on *incidents* in her life.

As her narrative illustrates, "Linda" has numerous opportunities to escape, but chooses to give up her freedom and her own life to save her children.

Jacobs was determined to convince the world of the devastating and dehumanizing impact of slavery on women, so she decided to document her horrific experiences as an enslaved African woman. Because she wanted to protect those individuals who might be hurt by her exposé, she assumed the pseudonym Linda Brent and, with the assistance of her editor, L. Maria Child, wrote what was to become one of the most powerful narratives of the slavery experience from a female perspective.

Slave Rebellions and Runaway Slaves

Many U.S. history books still contend that enslaved Africans were generally resigned to their fate and that slave revolts were rare and unusual occurrences. This attitude, which was common among slave-holders and those tasked with recording our nation's history, perpetuated the belief that slaves were generally passive and complacent and had no real reason or desire to rebel or to run away, a concept that more recent research has proven to be blatantly false.

Slave Rebellions

Historians estimate that more than 250 organized slave revolts and conspiracies took place in what is now U.S. territory, and thousands more occurred in the Caribbean and in Central and South America. The leaders of slave revolts were often seen as murderers and lunatics by whites. Among blacks, however, they were usually viewed as heroes and martyrs, although some slaves saw them as dangerous to their own survival. The most infamous slave revolts were those led by Gabriel Prosser, Denmark Vesey, and Nat Turner. Although all three men were ultimately apprehended and executed, their courage and daring inspired other blacks to fight for their freedom and to cling to the hope that they, too, would someday be free.

In 1800, Gabriel Prosser, a slave living on a plantation in southern Virginia, vowed to escape the brutal treatment of his master, Thomas Prosser. He organized a plot in which approximately 1,100 slaves were to take Richmond. Prosser envisioned that his "army" would eventually be joined by as many as 50,000 more. As the time for the revolt drew near, two of the slaves warned authorities of the plot. As a result, Prosser and 35 other slaves were executed, and the Prosser conspiracy gained national attention. Governor James Monroe described it as "unquestionably the most serious and formidable conspiracy we have ever known."

Several years later in South Carolina, Denmark Vesey, a slave who had purchased his freedom in 1800 with money from a winning lottery ticket, led another uprising. Vesey, who was a native of St. Thomas in the West Indies, worked as a carpenter in Charleston, South Carolina. Over a period of seven months, he planned an uprising to "liberate" the city, encouraging slaves to seize weapons, commandeer ships, and sail for the West Indies. Vesey's plot attracted more than 9,000 slaves and free blacks, but several slaves betrayed him, leading to the arrest of 131 blacks and four whites. In the end, at least 35 men, including Vesey, were executed.

By far the most notorious and successful slave rebellion was led by Nat Turner in Southampton County, Virginia, in 1831. Turner was born in Southampton County on October 2, 1800, the same year Prosser led his rebellion and Vesey was freed. Turner was raised by his mother and paternal grandmother after his father ran away, and he was 31 years old when he led his infamous rebellion, often called his *insurrection*.

Turner, who was the slave of Joseph Travis, was a preacher who saw visions and felt divinely inspired to lead his people to freedom. He plotted his revolt for six months, sharing his plan with only four others. On the day the revolt was to take place, he and his men gathered in the woods and then began their raid by attacking the Travis plantation and killing the entire family. By the following morning, Turner's group, which had grown to 60, had traveled through the county, killing at least 57 whites. As the revolt progressed, Turner's "army" continued to grow. They were finally stopped on their way to Jerusalem, the county seat, where they had hoped to gain additional support and replenish their ammunition. Thirteen slaves and three free blacks were hanged, but Turner was not captured until two months later, less than five miles from where the raid had begun.

Thomas R. Gray, a lawyer and plantation owner assigned as Turner's defense counsel, interviewed Turner during his trial and later published *The Confessions of Nat Turner*, a pamphlet containing the story of Turner's rebellion from his own point of view. (William Styron later wrote an award-winning novel by the same title, which drew much controversy from blacks who claimed it presented a totally distorted view of Turner.) Gray made no attempt to defend Turner and called no witnesses to testify on his behalf. As a result, Turner was hanged on November 11, 1831. His corpse was skinned and his flesh was used for grease.

Turner's revolt led to harsh laws throughout the South, further restricting the limited freedom of blacks. It also spurred blacks and abolitionists into action and increased tensions between the North and South.

Runaway Slaves

Instead of engaging in organized revolt, many slaves ran away in order to escape the bondage of slavery.

In their book *Runaway Slaves: Rebels on the Plantation* (New York: Oxford University Press, 1999), historians John Hope Franklin and Loren Schweninger explore this form of rebellion. Franklin and Schweninger describe three categories of runaways: *absentees* (slaves who left the plantation for a few days or weeks); *outlyers* (slaves who hid in the woods for months or even years); and *maroons* (slaves who established camps in remote swamps and bayous). The authors also discuss the role of "term slaves" (slaves who were to be set free at some future date) and free blacks, who sometimes helped others escape. According to the authors, the "typical" runaway was a young male plantation hand between the ages of 13 and 29.

One of the primary methods of escape for runaways was the infamous Underground Railroad, a secret network of blacks and whites that illegally helped fugitive slaves reach safety in the North or Canada. The network, also referred to as the "Liberty Line," used railroad terms to describe its operations. For example, guides were referred to as "conductors," hiding places were "stations," and groups of slaves were "trains." The "Liberty Line" generally ran from Virginia and Kentucky across Ohio, or from Maryland across Pennsylvania to New York, New England, and Canada.

From 1830 to 1860, it is estimated that nearly 9,000 fugitives passed through Philadelphia and nearly 40,000 through Ohio.

The most famous black conductor was Harriet Tubman, who was often compared to the biblical character of Moses because she made at least ten trips North over a period of ten years, leading more than 200 slaves to freedom.

In addition to running away, slaves also used more subversive tactics to escape slavery, such as self-mutilation and arson. And mothers sometimes killed themselves and their children to save them from slavery, as Jacobs alludes in her novel.

"We the People. . . ": Slavery and the U.S. Constitution

Although the U.S. Constitution (approved September 17, 1787) contains no *direct* references to slavery, it includes several *indirect* references to that "peculiar institution." The following are the references as well as translations of the legal language.

Article I, Section 2 . . . Representatives and direct Taxes shall be apportioned among the several States which may be included within this Union, according to their respective Numbers, which shall be determined by adding to the whole Number of free Persons, including those bound to Service for a Term of Years, and excluding Indians not taxed, three fifths of all other Persons. . . .

Translation: State representation and taxation will be based on the number of "free Persons" (whites) plus "three fifths of all other Persons" (blacks), implying that blacks are less than full human beings. This passage is generally referred to as the "three-fifths rule."

The passage was changed by Section 2 of the Fourteenth Amendment (ratified July 9, 1868): "Representatives shall be apportioned among the several States according to their respective numbers, counting the whole number of persons in each State, excluding Indians not taxed."

Article I, Section 9. The Migration or Importation of such Persons as any of the States now existing shall think proper to admit, shall not be prohibited by the Congress prior to the Year one thousand eight hundred and eight, but a Tax or duty may be imposed on such Importation, not exceeding ten dollars for each Person.

Translation: The "Importation" of certain persons (the slave trade) could be stopped after 1808. After that date, Congress could place a tax on anyone brought into the United States as a slave. This passage had a horrific impact on enslaved Africans, because slave traders would sometimes dispose of their "cargo" to avoid paying taxes.

Article IV, Section 2 . . . No Person held to Service or Labour in one State, under the Laws thereof, escaping into another, shall, in Consequence of any Law or Regulation therein, be discharged from such Service or Labour, but shall be delivered up on Claim of the Party to whom such Service or Labour may be due.

Translation: Anyone escaping from bondage into another state would be returned to his or her "owner." Before this law was passed, slaves were free if they could escape from a "slave" state to a "free" state. After the law was passed, enslaved blacks had to escape to Canada or Mexico to secure their freedom.

This passage was changed by Section 1 of the Thirteenth Amendment (ratified December 6, 1865): "Neither slavery nor involuntary servitude, except as a punishment for crime whereof the party shall have been duly convicted, shall exist within the United States, or any place subject to their jurisdiction."

In addition, amendments to the Constitution were required to enable blacks to serve in the U.S. Armed Forces, to integrate schools and other public facilities, and to enable blacks to exercise their right to vote. Clearly, then, the phrase "all men are created equal" did not apply to blacks, because the "founding fathers" perceived them as being less than human.

Slave Narrative Conventions

Incidents in the Life of a Slave Girl is a slave narrative, an autobiography (first-person narrative) by an enslaved black American woman who describes her experiences in slavery and her escape from bondage in the South to freedom in the North. The slave narrative is closely related to the memoir and the autobiography. (A *memoir* is generally defined as a form of autobiography that deals with the recollections of prominent people who have experienced or witnessed important events. Memoirs are usually concerned with the personalities and actions of others, but *autobiography* focuses on the writer's inner life.)

Because slave narratives document the horrors of slavery as experienced by ex-slaves, they serve as a powerful tool for exposing the brutalities of the chattel slave system, which defined people as "property." The narratives also served as a testament to the courage and dignity of black men and women who were perceived by their "masters" as subhuman creatures without souls.

Slave narratives first appeared in the United States around 1703, but most were published during the era of abolitionism, from 1831 to the end of the Civil War in 1865. One of the most prominent slave narratives published during this period was Frederick Douglass' *Narrative* (1845). Other narratives of this period include William Wells Brown's

Narrative of William W. Brown, Written by Himself; The Interesting Narrative of the Life of Olaudah Equiano, or Gustavas Vasa, the African; and *The History of Mary Prince: A West Indian Slave.*

After 1865, over 60 book-length narratives were published, including Booker T. Washington's *Up From Slavery*, and James Weldon Johnson's *The Autobiography of an Ex-Coloured Man.* Under the federal government's Work Projects Administration, the largest single group of slave narratives was collected. The collection—gathered in the South in the mid-1930s—includes 2,194 oral histories of elderly ex-slaves.

One of the defining characteristics of the slave narrative is the testimonial or letter of authenticity generally written by a white editor or abolitionist friend of the narrator. In order to be published, black authors had to be endorsed by whites who could testify to their credibility and the authenticity of their stories.

Another defining characteristic of the slave narrative is a phrase such as "Written by Herself" in the narrative's title, and an opening statement such as "I was born. . . ," followed by a place of birth, but no birth date.

The body of the narrative generally includes vague references to the narrator's parents, descriptions of a cruel master or overseer, descriptions of whippings and other brutal treatments, and accounts of slaves being sold on the auction block.

Other distinguishing characteristics of the slave narrative are its simple, forthright style; vivid characters; and striking dramatic incidents, particularly graphic violence and daring escapes, such as that by Henry "Box" Brown, who packed himself into a small crate and was shipped north to waiting abolitionists.

Slave narratives are patterned after the biblical story of the Jewish people's escape from bondage and their subsequent journey to the Promised Land. Consequently, slave narratives often assume a religious framework and explore several common themes, such as the quest for freedom, the search for home, redemption and salvation, the search for deliverance from evil, and the crossing of boundaries. For example, the biblical stories focused on the Jews' escape from tyrannical rule, their journey to the Promised Land, and their perilous crossings of the River Jordan and the Red Sea, but slave narratives focus on black people's escape from their often cruel masters on southern plantations, their journeys north, and their perilous crossings of the Ohio River en route to the Free States, a water passage that mirrors the horrific Middle Passage of enslaved Africans from Africa to North America.

Because slaves were legally denied the right to read and write, often under penalty of disfigurement or death, American slave narratives also focus on the quest for literacy, which was often linked with the quest for freedom. (Slaves who could read and write were more likely to escape, because they could forge their own passes and read about the successful escapes of other slaves.)

Like the Negro spirituals, slave narratives have had a profound impact on contemporary American literature. And like the spirituals—which often contain secret codes decipherable only by enslaved blacks—they were considered dangerous and subversive by slaveholders, who feared that they might incite slave revolts and riots.

A primary goal of the slave narratives was to gain the sympathy of white readers and gain support for the abolitionist movement.

CliffsNotes Review

Use this CliffsNotes Review to test your understanding of the original text, and reinforce what you've learned in this book. After you work through the fill-in-the-blank section, identify the quote, and review and essay questions, you're well on your way to understanding a comprehensive and meaningful interpretation of Jacobs' *Incidents in the Life of a Slave Girl.*

Identify the Quote

1. "I had my season of joy and thanksgiving. It was the first time since my childhood that I had experienced any real happiness. I heard of the old doctor's threats, but they no longer had the same power to trouble me. The darkest cloud that hung over my life had rolled away."

2. ". . . my heart was heavier than it had ever been before. Slavery is terrible for men; but it is far more terrible for women."

3. "They would begin to understand their own capabilities, and exert themselves to become men and women."

   Answers: (1) [Linda finds out that her children are no longer owned by Dr. Flint.] (2)[Linda responds to the discovery that her newly born baby is female.] (3) [Linda comments on what the results would be if slaves were given accurate knowledge. Linda laments the fact that slaves are not educated and are kept ignorant about the Free States and the possibilities of freedom. She believes that knowledge brings empowerment.]

Fill-in-the-Blank Questions

1. Linda Brent is a pseudonym for _____ _____.

2. In the Preface, Linda reveals that she spent _____ years as a slave.

3. After the death of her parents, Linda is raised by her grandmother, known in the white community as _____ _____.

4. Linda is only _____ years old when Dr. Flint begins to pursue her.

5. Determined to escape the relentless pursuit of Dr. Flint, Linda enters into a sexual relationship with _____.

6. Linda hides in her grandmother's garret for _____ years.

7. Linda refers to her hiding place as her "_____ __ _____."

8. Linda's children are named _____ and _____.

9. Linda's travels abroad with Mr. Bruce and his daughter, Mary, take her to _____.

10. The second Mrs. Bruce finally buys Linda's freedom for $_____.

Answers: (1) Harriet Jacobs. (2) 27. (3) Aunt Martha. (4) 15. (5) Mr. Sands. (6) 7. (7) loophole of retreat. (8) Benny and Ellen. (9) England. (10) 300.

Essay Questions

1. Jacobs' autobiography is accompanied by two advocacy letters attesting to the work's authenticity—one by Amy Post, a white Quaker abolitionist, the other by George W. Lowther, whom Brent's editor, Lydia Maria Child, identifies as "a highly respectable colored citizen of Boston." These testimonials reveal that had Brent succeeded in publishing the narrative on her own, readers would not have believed that it was written by a former slave. Given the relationship between the testimonials and the narrative, consider the following:

a. Does Brent's narrative live up to the expectations set by the testimonials?

b. Is the work as moving and dramatic as these writers say it is?

c. Does Brent's role as an observer of her own time, and as the author of her life's story, give her work credibility independent of what others say?

d. Could you argue that Brent's story is far superior to the material that supports it?

2. Does Brent's narrative support the concept that literacy is a metaphor for freedom? Explain.

3. Brent's relationship with her grandmother (Aunt Martha) gives her the strength to endure seemingly impossible hardships in order to be near her children. What impact do some of the other women in the narrative have on Brent's life?

4. The use of language is a critical factor in Brent's narrative. For example, numerous critics have pointed out that Brent's sophisticated manner of speaking seems incompatible with her character. Discuss.

5. Compare the opening chapter of *Incidents* with the opening chapter of Frederick Douglass's *Narrative*. What are some of the key differences between these two works?

6. Compare Brent's *Incidents* to Toni Morrison's *Beloved*. How does Morrison's graphic use of language to describe the horrors of slavery add to the emotional impact of her work?

7. In discussing the continuing problems of racism and the dismal social and economic status of inner-city blacks, historians often refer to "the legacy of slavery." Based on Brent's experiences as a slave and as a free woman in the United States, how valid are their observations?

8. In Chapter 1, "Childhood," Brent describes the "unusually fortunate circumstances" of her early childhood from ages 6-12, before she became fully aware of her slave status. With this in mind, read Zora Neale Hurston's essay, "How It Feels to Be Colored Me." How does Hurston's experience reflect Brent's?

9. When Aunt Martha tells Linda that her father is dead (Chapter 2), Linda recalls her initial response: "He had died so suddenly I had not even heard that he was sick." What does this incident reveal about Aunt Martha? About Linda? What are the circumstances surrounding her father's death? Why do you think Linda was not permitted to attend her father's funeral?

10. In Chapter 3, Brent describes the meaning of New Year's Day from a slave's perspective. With this in mind, read Frederick Douglass' speech, "What to the Slave is the Fourth of July." How is his message similar to Brent's?

11. In Chapter 4, "The Slave Who Dared to Feel Like a Man," Brent tells the story of her Uncle Benjamin. What impact does this story seem to have on her?

12. In Chapter 5, "The Trials of Girlhood," Brent relates the story of two sisters—one black, one white—and their very different fates. How does this story affect her personally?

13. In Chapter 6, "The Jealous Mistress," Brent describes the relationship between Dr. and Mrs. Flint. Based on her description, how would you characterize their marriage?

14. In Chapter 7, Linda describes her relationship with a free black man who offers to buy her freedom. How does this relationship affect her decision to enter into a sexual liaison with Mr. Sands?

15. In Chapter 8, Brent describes "What Slaves are Taught to Think of the North." What is the underlying message of this chapter?

16. In Chapter 9, Brent provides sketches of three slaveholders: Mr. Litch, Mr. Conant, and Mrs. Wade. How would you characterize these three individuals?

17. In Chapter 10, "A Perilous Passage in the Slave Girl's Life," Brent describes her relationship with Mr. Sands. How is her decision to enter into this relationship a "perilous passage" in her life?

18. By choosing to have two children by Mr. Sands, it can be argued that Brent is largely responsible for creating her own dilemma. Discuss.

19. In Chapter 11, Brent describes the birth of her son, Ben. How does this incident impact her life?

20. In Chapter 12, "Fear of Insurrection," Brent describes the aftermath of the Nat Turner Rebellion. Discuss.

21. In Chapter 13, "The Church and Slavery," Brent explores the moral conflict between slavery and Christianity. Does she build a successful case for the incompatibility of these two institutions? Discuss.

22. In Chapters 14–16, Brent describes the birth of her daughter, Ellen, and her experiences on Mr. Flint's plantation. How do these incidents affect her?

23. What is the significance of Brent's statement that "the colored race are the most cheerful and forgiving people on the face of the earth"?

24. In Chapters 17–20, Brent describes her first attempt to escape and the aftermath of her actions. Discuss.

25. Chapter 21, "The Loophole of Retreat," presents a pivotal point in Brent's story. Discuss.

26. What are some of the Christmas rituals and festivities Brent describes in Chapter 22?

27. In Chapter 25, "Competition in Cunning," Brent tricks Dr. Flint into thinking she is in New York by writing him a letter and having it postmarked in New York. Explore the connections between Brent's narrative and the "cunning" characters in black folktales such as "Br'er Rabbit" and "Big John."

28. In Chapter 35, "Prejudice Against Color," Brent explores the complex issue of color prejudice among some blacks, a prejudice that can be traced directly to the institution of slavery. Explain.

29. In Chapter 37, "A Visit to England," Brent compares her treatment in England with her treatment in the United States. How does she characterize her experiences?

30. In Chapter 40, "The Fugitive Slave Act," Brent discusses the impact of this law on runaway slaves. What were some of the issues that led to the passage of this law?

31. In Chapter 41, "Free at Last," Brent describes her experiences upon finally obtaining her freedom. But how "free" is she really? Cite examples from the text to support your argument. You may also want to research the passage of Jim Crow laws in the South.

CliffsNotes Resource Center

The learning doesn't need to stop here. CliffsNotes Resource Center shows you the best of the best—links to the best information in print and online about the author and/or related works. And don't think that this is all we've prepared for you; we've put all kinds of pertinent information at www.cliffsnotes.com. Look for all the terrific resources at your favorite bookstore or local library and on the Internet. When you're online, make your first stop www.cliffsnotes.com, where you'll find more incredibly useful information about Harriet A. Jacobs and *Incidents in the Life of a Slave Girl, Written by Herself.*

Books

This CliffsNotes book, published by IDG Books Worldwide, Inc., provides a meaningful interpretation of *Incidents in the Life of a Slave Girl.* If you are looking for information about the author and/or related works, check out these other publications:

The Classic Slave Narratives, Henry Louis Gates, Jr., Editor. Edited by renowned scholar and critic Henry Louis Gates, Jr. (with Nellie McKay) of *The Norton Anthology of African American Literature,* this compact paperback provides a comprehensive introduction to the slave narrative genre and the full text of four classic slave narratives: *The Interesting Narrative of the Life of Olaudah Equiano; The History of Mary Prince: A West Indian Slave; Narrative of the Life of Frederick Douglass;* and *Incidents in the Life of a Slave Girl.* New York: Penguin Books, 1987.

The Confessions of Nat Turner, Leader of the Late Insurrection in Southampton, Va. First published in 1861, this booklet is a reprint of Nat Turner's confessions, as recorded during a series of interviews by his attorney, Thomas C. Gray. The text is a transcript of Turner's statement concerning the insurrection, as read before the court of Southampton, convened for Turner's trial at Jerusalem, Virginia, November 5, 1831. Ayer Company Publishers, Inc., 1994.

Harriet Jacobs and Incidents in the Life of a Slave Girl, Deborah M. Garfield and Rafia Zafar, Editors. This text features 13 insightful essays by renowned critics and scholars that address issues such as female abolitionism, the politics of sex, redemption, motherhood, and civil disobedience. It is an indispensable resource for Jacobs scholars. Of special interest are the essays by Jacqueline Goldsby and Jean Fagan Yellin that explore the relationship between *Incidents* and "A True Tale," a narrative written by Jacobs's brother, John, that provides a male perspective of some of the incidents described by Jacobs in her narrative. New York: Cambridge University Press, 1996.

Incidents in the Life of a Slave Girl, Written by Herself. (2nd Edition.), by Harriet A. Jacobs, Jean Fagan Yellin, Editor. Edited by Jacobs' biographer, this definitive edition includes the full text of the original manuscript. Features include a detailed introduction that provides readers with an overview of the narrative and its unique place in U.S. history, literature, and culture, numerous illustrations, extensive annotations that clarify some of the more obscure passages of the text, a chronology of Jacobs' life, the names of the individuals represented in her narrative, and excerpts from Jacobs' personal letters. Cambridge, Mass: Harvard University Press, 2000.

Rebels Against Slavery: American Slave Revolts, by Patricia C. McKissack and Fredrick L. McKissack. A recent addition to the Scholastic series of young adult books, *Rebels Against Slavery* is a fact-filled, fascinating account of American slave revolts. The book is unique in that it depicts the rebel slaves such as Toussaint Louverture, Gabriel Prosser, Denmark Vesey, Nat Turner, and Cinque not as murderers and fanatics, but as heroic freedom fighters. Supplemented with numerous illustrations, an extensive bibliography, and a chronology of "Important Dates" in the history of slavery. New York: Scholastic Incorporated, 1996.

Runaway Slaves: Rebels on the Plantation, by John Hope Franklin and Loren Schweninger. This new work by renowned historian John Hope Franklin documents numerous accounts of slave resistance and rebellion. Features include profiles of "typical" runaways, numerous illustrations, an extensive bibliography and six detailed appendixes that provide excerpts from primary source documents such as letters, reward posters, and bills of sale. New York: Oxford University Press, 1999.

The Slave's Narrative, Charles T. Davis and Henry Louis Gates, Jr., Editors. This collection of essays and reviews by scholars and critics such as Sterling Brown, John Edgar Wideman, Robert Stepto, Houston A. Baker, Jr., and Jean Fagan Yellin (Jacobs' biographer) is an indispensable resource on slave narratives from a historical as well as literary perspective. Features include an extensive introduction on the language of slavery, numerous illustrations, and a bibliography of more than 100 slave narratives by Black Americans and African Muslims. New York: Oxford University Press, 1985.

Book Essays and Articles by Jean Fagan Yellin

"Text and Contexts of Harriet Jacobs' *Incidents in the Life of a Slave Girl: Written by Herself.*" *The Slave's Narrative.* Charles T. Davis and Henry Louis Gates, Jr., Editors. In this groundbreaking essay, Yellin—Jacobs' biographer—cites excerpts from Jacobs' personal correspondence that establish her authorship of *Incidents*, clarify the role of her editor, Lydia Maria Child, and link Jacobs with other 19th century figures such as Nathaniel P. Willis (Mr. Bruce), Harriet Beecher Stowe (*Uncle Tom's Cabin*), and abolitionist Amy Post. New York: Oxford University Press, 1985: 262–282.

"Through Her Brother's Eyes: *Incidents* and 'A True Tale.'" Deborah M. Garfield and Rafia Zafar, Editors. *Harriet Jacobs and Incidents in the Life of a Slave Girl.* Yellin contends that "A True Tale," a narrative by Jacobs' brother, John, authenticates Jacobs' narrative and offers a unique male perspective of the incidents described by his sister. New York: Cambridge University Press, 1996: 44–56.

Traditional Slave Narratives

Narrative of the Life of Frederick Douglass, an American Slave, Written by Himself, by Frederick Douglass. Signet, 1997.

Our Nig; or, Sketches from the Life of a Free Black, by Harriette Wilson. Random House, 1983.

Up From Slavery, by Booker T. Washington. Signet, 2000.

Contemporary Slave Narratives

The Autobiography of Malcolm X, by Malcolm X (with Alex Haley). New York: Random House, 1992 [1964].

Black Boy, by Richard Wright. New York: Harper Collins, 1993 [1944].

It's easy to find books published by IDG Books Worldwide, Inc. You'll find them in your favorite bookstores (on the Internet and at a store near you). We also have three web sites that you can use to read about all the books we publish:

- www.cliffsnotes.com

- www.dummies.com

- www.idgbooks.com

Internet

Check out this Web resource for more information about Harriet A. Jacobs and *Incidents in the Life of a Slave Girl, Written by Herself:*

Harriet Jacobs' Home Page, xroads.virginia.edu/~HYPER/ JACOBS/ hjhome.htm—includes a wealth of materials on Jacobs, including photographs, a chronology of Jacobs's life, and an extensive glossary.

Next time you're on the Internet, don't forget to drop by www.cliffsnotes.com. We created an online Resource Center that you can use today, tomorrow, and beyond.

Films and Other Recordings

Africans in America: America's Journey Through Slavery. This powerful PBS video series tells the story of America through the eyes of enslaved Africans. Background materials were drawn from original source materials and the latest scholarship on slavery. The series consists of four parts: "Terrible Transformation: 1607–1750"; "Revolution: 1750–1805"; "Brotherly Love: 1787–1834"; and "Judgment Day: 1831–1861."

Magazines and Journals

Yellin, Jean Fagan. "Written by Herself: Harriet Jacobs' Slave Narrative." *American Literature*, Nov. 1981: 53 (3): 479–86. In this essay, Yellin describes the process she went through to establish the authenticity of Jacobs's narrative.

Send Us Your Favorite Tips

In your quest for knowledge, have you ever experienced that sublime moment when you figure out a trick that saves time or trouble? Perhaps you realized that you were taking ten steps to accomplish something that could have taken two. Or you found a little-known workaround that achieved great results. If you've discovered a useful tip that helped you understand *Incidents in the Life of a Slave Girl* more effectively and you'd like to share it, the CliffsNotes staff would love to hear from you. Go to our Web site at www.cliffsnotes.com and click the Talk to Us button. If we select your tip, we may publish it as part of CliffsNote-A-Day, our exciting, free e-mail newsletter. To find out more or to subscribe to a newsletter, go to www.cliffsnotes.com on the Web.

Index

NOTES

NOTES

NOTES

NOTES

NOTES

Check Out the All-New CliffsNotes Guides

TECHNOLOGY TOPICS

PERSONAL FINANCE TOPICS

CAREER TOPICS